CHEATS, CHOICES & DUMBING DOWN

A BOOK ABOUT EXAMS FOR

PUSHY PARENTS, STREETWISE STUDENTS AND TIRELESS TEACHERS

JERRY JARVIS &
GARY WARD

Published by Pukka Publications February 2012

ISBN: 978-0-9570842-0-9

Publisher's Note
Every effort has been made to ensure that the information in this book is accurate at the time of going to press and has been set out in good faith for general guidance. The publishers and authors cannot accept any responsibility or liability for any loss or expense as a result of acting upon, or refusing to act, as a result of statements made in the book. Education and exams policy is subject to change and readers should check the current position before making personal arrangements.

For more information, to learn more and keep up to date, *see: www.examlinks.co.uk.*

References to Ofqual source data is in accordance with: Ofqual, 2011. Licensed under the Open Government Licence.

ACKNOWLEDGEMENTS

I t was a great privilege to work with people who serve education. There is dedication and a passion in education that is rarely found elsewhere. My respect and admiration goes to my former colleagues in Edexcel and in the Pearson Organisation; my competitors in AQA, CCEA, City and Guilds, OCR and WJEC; the staff of the regulators and the education departments; the Joint Council for Qualifications; the Federation of Awarding Bodies; the Association of Colleges, and a myriad of educational organisations, pressure groups and charities that are too numerous to mention here. I thank the teachers and professionals who tolerated my interventions in the world of assessment and who so professionally delivered the judgements that underpin the success of our qualifications.

Finally, may I also thank the pupils, parents, students and adult learners who take exams and qualifications in their millions and to whom this book is dedicated.

TABLE OF CONTENTS

About the authors   1

Foreword   3

Chapter 1: You may turn over your papers and begin. How the exam system works   11

Chapter 2: The Qualifications: GCSE   27

Chapter 3: The Qualifications: A-level (or GCE)   41

Chapter 4: Other Qualifications: the good, the bad and the ugly   51

Chapter 5: Which subjects should you choose?   63

Chapter 6: How to achieve better results   83

Chapter 7: Cheat! How cheating is done, how it's spotted – and the consequences of getting caught   101

Chapter 8: 'Exams are getting easier.' Discuss   119

Chapter 9: On your marks... How exams are marked and graded   141

Chapter 10: Results day and beyond   157

Chapter 11: In conclusion. Where do we go from here?   169

ABOUT THE AUTHORS

Jerry Jarvis left his very successful appointment as Managing Director of Edexcel to 'put something back' into education and has since helped many people and organisations, particularly in the charity sector. Jerry is an engineer with formidable experience in business improvement and has pioneered a number of scientific and operational breakthroughs during a long career in the manufacturing and customer service sectors. He is a keen photographer and musician.

Gary Ward runs a consultancy dedicated to helping companies, organisations and individuals to get their message across and communicate better. A former journalist, he has worked for many education clients and also has experience in health, social care, criminal justice and other fields. He has two children at secondary school, one of whom was studying for GCSEs while he helped to write this book.

FOREWORD

This book is about the exam system in England, Wales and Northern Ireland. Our exams are very complicated and even teachers sometimes find them remote and confusing. Educators often cloak what they do in difficult language and habitually disagree with one another. The situation is made worse by the media – newspapers and TV – as they respond to our anxieties by constant accusations that exams are getting easier. We are told that we are 'dumbing down' our education. So are the GCSEs, A-levels and BTECs worth the paper that they are written on? Well, I have a strong interest here because my authorising signature appears on millions of GCSE, A-level and BTEC certificates, and I know the answers to the questions about exam standards and dumbing down. I ran the largest and most successful exam board in the country and I know the people who set and mark exams. In 2009 I met with the then Chair and Chief Executive of the exams regulator, Ofqual, and resigned the authority that empowered me to authorise exam certificates. I will tell you why in chapter 8; you might be surprised by what I have to say.

I have tried to avoid offering personal opinions on government policy and on curriculum content in schools and colleges. Instead I have concentrated on helping those who use the exam system to understand it better and challenge it to their advantage. The way exams are run is changing and making choices about which exams to take and what subjects to select might well become even more important than in the past. Are some subjects easier than others? What you read here may make you think again. Use this book to gain an insight into the workings of the exam programme. It could help you, your students, pupils or children to get the best from the hard work expended in preparation for the big day; and it will guide you on what to do when things go wrong.

I wrote this book because I want you to have a greater say in the way that exams are set and run. I want you to be able to challenge the grades that are awarded if you suspect that they are incorrect. I will explain how some students get more time in the exam room or have their marks increased after the exam has been taken. I will give you access to the rules that are used by exam boards and will help you to understand why they behave the way that they do. I think that we, as parents, teachers and students, should take a leaf from the book of consumerism. We should expect more from the system that evaluates us. It should be transparent, accurate and repeatable. It should adopt modern technology and thinking. Most of all it should deliver qualifications and examination certificates that we can trust.

There is a great deal in our education system to be very proud of. The overwhelming majority of teachers, regulators, civil servants and exam board staff work with a high degree of integrity. Our exam programme is basically very honest, despite the enormous pressure on everyone to succeed. These days, the exam system gets the basics done reasonably well: new papers are written, kept secret and delivered on time; question papers are marked by the required deadlines – and we get our results issued on schedule. However, our exam system is outdated. We rely on expert opinion and judgement, and it is very difficult to get improvements adopted. There is a saying that if a teacher was somehow transported through time from a classroom in the distant past, the teacher would be shocked by the interactive whiteboard and student behaviour, but would quickly settle into the routine of teaching the class. The process of assessing students by written exam also looks much as it did many years ago. Of course subject matter and expectations have moved on, but the same old procedure persists. Few teachers are aware of the potential that technology can offer to improve teaching and learning.

In 2002 I began to develop new ways of running exams and marking student papers with better accuracy and consistency. I introduced digital technology that had been proven to work in mainstream industry to make groundbreaking improvements. I electronically scanned completed student exam papers so that they could be marked online and demonstrated improved integrity and accuracy. Luck was on my side. A radical educationalist,

Ken Boston, was appointed to head up the regulator and he opened the door to change for a few brief years.

My entry into the world of education was accidental. I have never taught in a school and I have no teaching qualifications. Indeed, before the year 2000 my only association with education was as a student. Up to that time I had spent most of my professional life as a senior manager or director in mainstream industry. I call myself an engineer, although I have been a director of operations, production, quality assurance, IT, design and procurement. I am lucky to have had a long formal education and to have worked with some great leaders. Throughout my working life I've had some successes of which I am very proud, although I do have the rare and dubious record of having set a nuclear submarine on fire.

During much of the 1990s I was a director of business change, helping to transform organisations. I worked with and for the best, including Marconi, BAe Systems and Thorn-EMI. My apparent ability to lead business transformation came to the notice of the exam board, Edexcel, which was undergoing reorganisation. I joined Edexcel during the summer exams in July 2000. The world of education is unique, and it took some time for me to adjust. I had become used to working in organisations that were described as world class. I was alarmed by the poor quality of the service that exam boards (or more accurately, Awarding Bodies) provided to schools and colleges. I was also deeply concerned by the poor administration of exams inside many schools and colleges. The management of exams programmes in the year 2000 was characterised by institutional failure across every aspect of activity. Worse, the most important people in the exams programme, the students, had no real voice in what was a faceless bureaucracy.

What I saw in the running of the exams in the year 2000 would not have been tolerated in any commercial enterprise. In a typical summer, exam boards, schools and colleges deal with about 250 million student responses to questions and assignments; 50,000 examiners have to be recruited and trained each time, and 20,000 telephone calls are made daily. Exams are a major operational task and they were being run by little groups of people who had rarely left the staff room. Perhaps the most difficult professional issue that I had to deal with was that of setting standards. In this book I have described how exam grades are set and you might well find the process unsettling; it relies wholly on experts who by simply looking at a student's effort can say whether it is worth a grade 'B' or 'C' and so on. Grades are ultimately determined by the opinion of a committee, not by facts, even for a subject like Maths. The engineer in me found the lack of a reliable, external reference difficult to accept.

About the time that I joined Edexcel, Curriculum 2000 was being introduced by the government. This brought significant structural changes to exams, including coursework and separate modules sat throughout the year instead of a single, final written exam paper. These changes caused havoc in a system already under severe pressure to deliver accurate exam results on time. Edexcel struggled to deal with 400,000 students entered for exams by schools and colleges more than two weeks late, and 30,000 students with duplicate identity numbers allocated by overwhelmed exams officers in schools. Chronic shortages of suitable teachers to mark the exams caused delays that led to results being late. Exam boards came under heavy criticism from the press and Edexcel was often singled out as incompetent.

These events caused many changes inside Edexcel and eventually resulted in my appointment as Managing Director. Around this time Edexcel was acquired by the Pearson Group, making it the only non-charitable organisation participating directly in the exam system. I will spare you the details, but in the years that followed a very professional management team was built and the entire exams programme was reformed. Edexcel probably undertakes the human assessment of students more accurately than any organisation in the world, using technologies that are exceptional. A visit to the company's data capture centre would astound you.

So, despite the trials and tribulations, this is a happy book. Our qualifications still enjoy international respect and we can be proud of the achievements of our students. But bureaucracy and lack of accountability are still strong in education. Use this book to help you to understand the way that it works and to get the best from it. The web site *www.examlinks.com* will take you directly to lots of very useful additional sources of information.

I could not have produced this book without the collaboration and contribution of the brilliant communications expert, Gary Ward. We wrote it together.

Jerry Jarvis

Chapter 1

YOU MAY TURN OVER YOUR PAPERS AND BEGIN

How the exam system works

For many people exams are a bit like going to the dentist – something you'd rather not do, but can't avoid. At school and college we assume that the exams we take fit into a grand plan. But later in life we see that exams and qualifications come and go; some become obsolete while others seem to last forever. As an adult, the number of different qualifications seems endless and choosing the right one can be difficult. If you're an employer, how can you understand what each qualification is really worth? If you're a teacher or school governor, keeping up with change places more and more demands on your time.

In this chapter I will take you on a journey through the exam system in England, Wales and Northern Ireland. For convenience I'll refer to this as the *English system*, with apologies to any offended Welsh and Northern Ireland citizens. Scotland has its own set of qualifications and exam authorities, although it is possible to study for and take English exams there and in most other countries in the world.

Government Policy – For Better or For Worse

If you think the current system is daft you're in good company, but why is it so complicated? Let's start with government policy, going back about 25 years to the creation of the national curriculum under Margaret Thatcher. This was meant to unify what was taught in schools. Has it worked? Not everyone thinks so. The academic, Professor Alison Wolf, gave a lecture in 2008 entitled: *'The national curriculum is outdated and no longer fit for purpose'*. She poured scorn on the exam system, and as an adviser to the present government, her views count.

Before the national curriculum existed, universities ran independent exam boards and schools taught different things, with few agreed standards. But in attempting to standardise what was taught, the new regime created a new bureaucracy. An organisation then called the Qualifications and Curriculum Authority (QCA) was set up to work with the Department for Children, Schools and Families (DCSF) to decide what should be taught in schools and colleges. But a word of warning here: the national curriculum is being reviewed by the re-named Department for Education (DfE) and many changes are under way. The Standards and Testing Agency now oversees exams from early years to the end of Key Stage Three, up to age 14. The exams regulator, Ofqual, is reviewing its role in overseeing exams.

All of this may lead to the list of subjects that can be taught in schools and colleges being changed significantly. This is important whatever your age. If you study a subject or qualification that may become obsolete, then it might reduce in value. For example, the last Labour government launched a flagship qualification called the Diploma, but it has had limited take-up, variable success and might disappear altogether. Qualifications have a 'brand' with some held in high esteem, and you should think about the value of a qualification before embarking on a course of study, so choose carefully. The latest thinking is for a new English Baccalaureate, but that has also attracted criticism and the Baccalaureate is not actually a qualification; it is a list of preferred, traditional subjects, which contribute significantly to school league table points in order to encourage schools to teach them.

Ofqual, the exams regulator, is a major player; this is how it describes itself:

"At Ofqual, we're responsible for maintaining standards, improving confidence and distributing information about qualifications and examinations. We regulate general and vocational qualifications in England and vocational qualifications in Northern Ireland. We give formal recognition to bodies and organisations that deliver qualifications and assessments. We also accredit their awards and monitor their activities (including their fees). We're not directly controlled by the government but report to parliament."

You can see it is a complex system. A crucial task carried out by Ofqual is to approve some of the organisations that play an important role in the exam system and to approve each new qualification offered, although the separate approval of each qualification might be discontinued in the future.

Ofqual's role is also changing. It is now being asked to make international comparisons with exam systems around the world to ensure we keep pace with our competitors.

THE NATIONAL CURRICULUM – A CREDIT OR A CURSE?

Most countries have a national curriculum and most people seem to agree that one is needed, but since it was introduced in 1986, it has probably had more rebrands than Madonna. It remains an area of fierce debate. In the words of Steve Besley, Pearson UK's Head of Policy:

"The national curriculum has become part mirror, reflecting the latest anxieties or concerns that society feels need tackling through schools, and part shopping list to which the latest flavour of the day is routinely added."

The national curriculum was meant to ensure that everyone was taught more or less the same thing, whether they lived in Newcastle or Newquay, Manchester or Margate. It was never meant to be too rigid, but just how flexible it is has been a bone of contention ever since. It was meant to make schools more accountable, enabling parents to compare school performance in their local area and with a national average. The introduction of league tables was a key factor here, letting everyone see how their local schools measured up. When it was introduced, all the talk was of a 'free market' in education – giving parents the information they needed to choose the best schools. In practice, league tables have meant that schools are judged by the number of good GCSE passes their pupils obtain; 'good' meaning grades A* to C.

Interestingly, the 'free market' has taken a twist with the introduction and growing numbers of free schools and academies. These don't have to follow the national curriculum, but do have to offer a "broad and balanced" education. However, their exam results will be published so parents and others will be able to compare their performance with other schools.

Few things, with the possible exception of national curriculum tests (known by most people as 'SATs'), get teaching unions quite so collectively red in the face as league tables. Combine this with Ofsted inspections and you have a recipe for a 'Big Brother' approach to schooling – according to the unions. Independent schools, it should be noted, are exempt from the national curriculum and can do pretty much what they like. This often seems to be voicing an opinion about how bad it is, despite it having nothing to do with them. Dr Martin Stephen, High Master of St Paul's, one of the UK's most exclusive private schools, has been quoted as saying:

"GCSE league tables are a complete work of fiction. They are actually becoming worse than a fiction and are becoming a straightforward lie." Ouch!

But the state sector doesn't have much time for league tables either, and they might be on their way out as government policy develops. Current thinking is focusing on an English Baccalaureate, which measures how many pupils in a school gain five good GCSE passes in Mathematics, English, a Science, a Foreign Language and a Humanities subject. Other factors, such as the overall quality of care in a school, may also be taken into account.

But the national curriculum isn't just another piece of jargon to be chewed over and spat out by teachers, unions, academics and government. It has a major say in what children must currently learn at school, dictating what has to be studied. For example, all pupils in state secondary schools must study, or learn about, Citizenship, English, ICT, Maths, PE and Science. In years 10 and 11, children must also be given careers advice, work-related learning and religious education, none of which is examined (unless Religious Studies is chosen as an option).

The government is also keen that school children show a grasp of so-called 'functional' skills. These promote the concepts of 'competence' and 'critical understanding', but also focus on Maths, English and ICT. The government has produced 52 pages of turgid guidance about functional skills alone if you'd really like to know more!

THE MARKET PLACE IN EXAMS

The way examinations are run in England is unique. Believe it or not, exams are bought and sold in a market place. The thinking behind it goes like this: if different organisations compete to develop good teaching materials and well-run exams, the quality of what is taught will improve as schools and colleges choose the best on offer. Like any other product, the competition is based on price, quality, customer service and other factors.

The regulator, Ofqual, licences suitable organisations to create exams within strict rules. This is known as 'recognition', and two types of recognition exist; one for academic qualifications like A-levels, GCSEs and Diplomas (known in this world as 'general qualifications'), and one for vocational qualifications. About 120 organisations are recognised providers of vocational qualifications, but only a handful are recognised to provide general qualifications.

Recognised organisations sell 'products' such as courses, textbooks and exams to schools, colleges and any other organisation that offers teaching and learning. The government gives schools and colleges money to buy these products, but lets them choose from whom to buy in the market place. Ofqual tries to ensure that we end up with a standard set of high quality qualifications, with market pressures driving innovation and efficiency. Sounds good? Well the current government doesn't think so and is planning to make changes all round. The market place has raised concern in some quarters that competition amongst exam boards fuels a 'race to the bottom' and that boards produce easy questions and offer increasing levels of support to teachers who buy their exams.

There's evidence that the brightest students are driven to take large numbers of exams and the not-so-bright discouraged. That explains why some students take as many as 12 or more GCSEs when up to nine is considered sensible.

Why? Because teachers are often under pressure to get the best results and highest league table position possible. Some do this by selecting 'GCSE equivalent' exams. Ofqual compares the 'value' of different qualifications and defines the 'GCSE equivalent' ratings for those that count towards league tables. They include vocational qualifications, such as BTECs and OCR Nationals, from the Edexcel and OCR exam boards – see chapter 4 for more on these. If the pass rates are higher in these alternative qualifications (and they usually are) then students can be switched from GCSE to these alternatives to boost the league table score. Other qualifications can also be manipulated to maximise league table points. The government is well aware of this and you can expect the list of GCSE equivalent qualifications to be slashed in the future.

Several other organisations have a hand in the exams and qualifications market place, including Sector Skills Councils, who advise government on what should be taught to support UK industry and commerce.

THE ROLE OF EXAM BOARDS

A word here about exam boards, or to give them their proper name, Awarding Organisations. They see what is compulsory or popular and develop the courses that contain what is to be learnt and how it is to be assessed. They also develop and sell support materials, such as books and teaching aids. Almost without exception, they only create qualifications that attract government funding, whether for academic or vocational needs.

With qualifications like A-levels and GCSEs the exam boards compete fiercely for market share, spending big money on development, advertising and promotion. This is a large market, worth well over £300m in direct sales to schools and colleges. The market is dominated by the three largest exam boards: AQA, Edexcel and OCR. They have to be mindful of any possible changes in funding, since withdrawal of funding for a qualification or subject would mean that schools and colleges would no longer buy it. Developing a new qualification is costly and can take 18 months as the materials go through the agonising bureaucracy needed to gain approval (although this bureaucracy is also under review).

Ofqual provides a list comparing the relative costs and features of different exam boards to help teachers choose the best supplier for them – a sort of comparison website for exam boards. Yet curious behaviour has emerged over the years. When schools and colleges decide which exam board to buy from, the decision is rarely made by the head teacher for the whole school. Instead, each subject head chooses the exam board, so each school or college's head of Geography may choose the course from one exam board, while the head of Maths chooses another, and so on. Incredibly, many buy from as many as four different general qualifications exam boards and 20 different vocational qualifications providers. This creates a bureaucratic nightmare for school administrators.

And there's a really interesting fact about this market place. In surveys, teachers say that price is one of the least important considerations when choosing the exam board. Higher on the agenda are questions like 'Will it be interesting?' 'Will it support progression to the next level?' 'Will my students be able to tackle the language used in the question papers'; and, most importantly, 'if I change exam board will my students perform less well because of my unfamiliarity with the new material?'

Later in this book I will look at how teachers actually decide which exam board to choose. Of course no teacher would ever admit to choosing an exam board on the basis of 'easiness' but the fact is that teachers tend not to shop around. The fear of a drop in pass rates following the adoption of a new and unfamiliar course tends to maintain loyalty to the current exam board. Added to this the regulator, Ofqual, has maintained that standards are upheld year-on-year. Nevertheless there is a worry amongst many in education and in government that competition is somehow causing problems. Some have called for a single provider of exams, as in Scotland.

WHAT ABOUT THE QUALITY?

If you are deciding which qualification to go for yourself, or are advising a son or daughter, you need to know about 'levels'. Levels indicate the degree of difficulty so that different qualifications can be compared. You might think this could be done with a simple list, but you'd be wrong. In the world of education, we have not one but two lists – see Figure 1.

The National Qualifications Framework (NQF) contains the academic qualifications, like GCSEs and A-levels, and the Qualifications and Credit Framework (QCF) contains the vocational qualifications, like BTECs, although the QCF could well be changed following a government review of vocational education.

It's supposed to be helpful, but it can be impossible to tell what level a particular qualification is at unless you read the lists very carefully. Who would have thought that a qualification entitled *Skills for Life at Level One* would be listed as a level 2 qualification? So when you are confronted by a leaflet, brochure, website, teacher or lecturer telling you that your intended qualification is at a particular level, look up the table.

I also need to mention 'tiers'. Exam boards provide some GCSE subjects with two different levels of difficulty, or tiers. In a higher tier exam you could receive any grade according to your performance – from A* to G, with the risk of not receiving a grade at all if you fall below the standard of Grade G. But in a foundation tier exam paper you can only be awarded a grade from C to G. This is important. Even if you scored 100% in a foundation tier GCSE paper, your grade would be 'C' and you might not be able to go on to A-level. The system is designed to enable less able students to sit a GCSE paper.

You might wonder why exam boards produce results by issuing grades rather than just telling you the mark you achieved out of a possible total. The reason is that different exams have different possible total scores – out of 100 or out of 70, for example. To make matters worse, consider three competing exam boards, each offering the same subject, setting their exam papers with different possible totals. The system has to be able to award similar performance equally and fairly.

Level	Examples of NQF qualifications	Examples of QCF qualifications
Entry	• Entry level certificates • English for Speakers of Other Languages (ESOL) • Skills for Life • Functional Skills at entry level (English, Maths and ICT)	• Awards, Certificates, and Diplomas at entry level • Foundation Learning at entry level • Functional Skills at entry level
1	• GCSEs grades D-G • BTEC Introductory Diplomas and Certificates • OCR Nationals • Key Skills at level 1 • Skills for Life • Functional Skills at level 1	• BTEC Awards, Certificates, and Diplomas at level 1 • Functional Skills at level 1 • Foundation Learning Tier pathways • NVQs at level 1
2	• GCSEs grades A*-C • Key Skills level 2 • Skills for Life • Functional Skills at level 1	• BTEC Awards, Certificates, and Diplomas at level 2 • Functional Skills at level 2 • OCR Nationals • NVQs at level 2

3	• A-levels • GCE in applied subjects • International Baccalaureate • Key Skills level 3	• BTEC Awards, Certificates, and Diplomas at level 3 • BTEC Nationals • OCR Nationals • NVQs at level 3
4	• Certificates of Higher Education	• BTEC Professional Diplomas Certificates and Awards • HNCs • NVQs at level 4
5	• HNCs and HNDs • Other Higher Diplomas	• HNDs • BTEC Professional Diplomas, Certificates and Awards • NVQs at level 5
6	• National Diploma in Professional Production Skills • BTEC Advanced Professional Diplomas, Certificates and Awards	• BTEC Advanced Professional Diplomas, Certificates and Awards
7	• Diploma in Translation • BTEC Advanced Professional Diplomas, Certificates and Awards	• BTEC Advanced Professional Diplomas, Certificates and Awards
8	• Specialist awards	• Award, Certificate and Diploma in Strategic Direction

Figure 1 Source: Ofqual

In summary, we have a national curriculum that defines what is to be taught and a regulator to ensure a level playing field in the market place for exams. We have a shortlist of approved exam bodies for general qualifications, a long list of approved organisations for vocational qualifications and an extremely long list of approved qualifications.

This system is expensive to run and league tables have significantly affected what is taught. But what of future needs? Will the curriculum deliver the learning necessary for our economic wellbeing? Will the Sector Skills Councils make the right investments in new training, and will our education system be able to keep up with the ferocious rate of technological change? It is hard to argue for a completely free system where what is taught and how it is assessed is left to professional teachers alone. We have become used to the notion that we can measure our national performance and it will be difficult to let that knowledge go. As the government implements changes in the years ahead we can expect financial pressures to reduce choice. Some qualifications will disappear and new qualifications may arrive. An exam system supported by fewer quangos should be simpler. In this changing world it is more important than ever to choose the right qualifications; ones that will not be made obsolete, and to get the best grades that you can.

One final change that could have a significant impact on exams is the introduction of free schools. These are independent of local authorities and have greater freedom to allocate the funding that they get from central government. Their independence might influence their choices of subjects and exam boards and lead to changes in the popularity of different qualifications. Free schools are intended to raise academic standards through competition and are based closely on the successful Swedish free school experience. However, Swedish school competition is based on commercial factors and they can make profits, underpinning the need for excellence in student performance. Anders Hultin, the man widely recognised as the expert in Swedish free schools, has said that financial competition is essential if free schools are to be successful. English free schools are (so far) not allowed to be run on a profit-making basis, and the deputy prime minister has reinforced this view.

QUICK REFERENCE: WHO'S WHO IN THE EXAM SYSTEM?

The Government

The Department for Education (DfE) – has the final say on education matters. In Wales and Northern Ireland, the devolved assemblies have a similar, strategic role.

The Standards and Testing Agency (STA) is a new body in England, based within the DfE, responsible for the testing and assessment of pupils up to 14.

The role of developing the curriculum and reviewing existing qualifications has been divided up between the DfE and the exam boards.

The Regulators

Ofqual (England), DFES (Wales), CCEA (Northern Ireland) – approve courses, maintain standards and regulate the exam boards.

The Exam Boards

Five major exam boards offer GCSEs and A Levels: Edexcel, AQA, OCR, WJEC and CCEA. One other very small specialist provider, ICCA, also exists. The exam boards develop the syllabus for each course, support teachers, write and mark the exam papers and compete with each other for schools' and colleges' business.

The Sector Skills Councils

Employer-led, UK-wide organisations, they have a say in what skills and knowledge is needed for our long term prosperity. Twenty two of them cover about 90% of the economy. Funding for these agencies is being withdrawn and their role will change significantly.

Chapter 2

THE QUALIFICATIONS: GCSE

During a period of massive change in the world of education, GCSEs have been a constant for almost 25 years. If you're aged 40 or less, you've probably taken some yourself, or if you're 14-16, the chances are you're studying for a number of them right now. Every year thousands of adults attend evening classes or take distance learning courses to gain GCSE qualifications. In the summer of 2011, 5,151,970 candidates sat full GCSEs, with almost a quarter achieving a grade A* or A. Today, more than 70 subjects are available, alongside 13 applied GCSEs, from the hardy perennials of Maths, English and History to the freshly minted Construction, Social Care and Hospitality.

GCSEs are part of the national curriculum. In the language of the educational establishment, a GCSE gained at grades D to G is classed as a 'level 1' qualification, while grades A* to C are 'level 2'.

THE ORIGINS OF GCSE

So where did it all begin? The General Certificate of Secondary Education (GCSE) was introduced by a

Conservative Government in 1986, with the first exams in 1988. The then Secretary of State for Education, Sir Keith Joseph, announced the change in 1984, saying:

"The system we propose will be tougher, but clearer and fairer. It will be more intelligible to users, better than O-levels, and better than CSE. It will stretch the able more and stretch the average more."

GCSEs in numbers

1986 – The year GCSEs were introduced

1988 – The year of the first GCSE exams

2002 – 5,662,382 entries, 16.4% gain grade A* or A

2005 – 5,736,505 entries with 18.4% at grade A* or A; and 18% at grade B

2008 – Entries hit a five year low of 5,669,077; 20.7% gain grade A* and A; 19.8% gain grade B

2010 – 5,3374,490, 22.6% gaining grade A* or A; and 20.6% gaining grade B

2010 – Chemistry and Physics entries up over 30% from 2009

70+ – The number of GCSE subjects available

13 – The number of GCSEs in applied subjects

Source: Joint Council for Qualifications

When the decision was announced, it was broadly welcomed by those pleased to see the back of the old two tier system of GCE O-levels and CSEs. The new qualification standardised exams and put all pupils into the same group of seven possible grades, A to G. It seems incredible now, but in those days there were 29 different exam boards, which were merged into five groups as a result of the changes. As recent calls for a single exam board are heard it might be interesting to see whether the dissenting voices come from the same people who campaigned for the retention of the old university boards. The old General Certificate of Education 'Ordinary' level had been the qualification of choice for pupils and parents until then; if you received a grade A, B or C, then you had passed an O-level. A grade D or E wasn't officially called a fail, but it was as good as failure and employers and colleges regarded it as such. For those who did really badly there was a 'U' or 'Unclassified' grade – that was right off the Richter scale of badness.

Before GCSEs were introduced, the other qualification taken at school was the Certificate of Secondary Education (CSE). Officially, this was for pupils whose academic performance was worse than their peers and who weren't thought bright enough to take O-levels. CSEs were graded on a scale of 1 to 5, with a grade 1 the equivalent of an O-level pass at grade C or above; so if you got a CSE grade 1, it was like passing an O-level - although of course it wasn't an O-level. O-levels were very important if you wanted to go on to study A-levels and have a chance of going to university. (There were exceptions; even Cambridge would accept CSE for certain courses).

One crucial element of the change was the way grades were awarded. The old system measured each candidate's performance against the others', but GCSEs changed all that. For the first time grades were awarded according to so-called 'absolute' standards. This is the root of the current 'dumbing down' debate.

A problem with the new GCSE exam was that gaps in ability hadn't just vanished with the morning mist. What would happen to those incapable of passing an O-level? The answer was that whilst the new GCSE was uniform in name, it most certainly was not uniform in nature. There were divisions from the start to account for different ability levels. As young people went through their secondary education and grew into adolescents, their ability was assessed and they were destined to take GCSE exams at either a higher or foundation tier. The higher tier GCSEs lead to a grade A* to G, while foundation tier exams lead to grades C to G – so if you or your son or daughter is entered for a foundation tier paper, the highest possible grade you can expect is a C. Most universities require five GCSE passes at grade A* to C, including Maths and English, in addition to A-levels or equivalent. You should be aware of the tier you are being entered for in each subject, although not all subjects have tiers, including Physical Education and Art.

WHAT ARE GCSES ACTUALLY FOR?

According to Ofqual, the exams regulator, any qualification, including the GCSE, "...is intended to show employers, teachers and learners what someone has learnt and can do as a result of that achievement." Fair enough, but, assuming you pass your GCSEs, you might also pick any of the following:

- ✓ It's a broad and well understood measure of achievement
- ✓ It provides the level of knowledge and understanding of each subject appropriate to the end of compulsory education
- ✓ It indicates a solid grounding in any subject, enabling students to specialise at a higher, more difficult, level
- ✓ It illustrates what skills you have developed to help in further study, at work and in life.

The skills learnt depend on the subject, but may include the ability to write an error-free sentence, solve a mathematical equation, write a piece of software or play a musical instrument. The government also says that the national curriculum for 14-16 year olds – when they're studying their GCSEs – should help young people to become successful learners, confident individuals and responsible citizens. I don't know about you, but that seems to be quite a big ask of any set of exams – although I suppose it depends how well you've done. Despite the critics and the growing number of alternatives, GCSEs remain the main way of assessing attainment at the end of compulsory education for 16 year olds in England, Wales and Northern Ireland, and they are a good foundation for formal learning in later life.

COURSEWORK OF COURSE

Over the years, new GCSE subjects have been introduced and the way they are marked and assessed has changed. One important change ushered in with the brave new world of GCSEs was coursework. For years, many teachers, academics, students and parents had argued that the 'all or nothing' end of year exams weren't fair. Some children (and grown-ups) panicked or were wracked with nerves and didn't perform anywhere near to the best of their ability in exams. Debates persist about whether exams really test knowledge and understanding – or rather an ability to pass exams.

The arguments in favour of having some way of measuring, and rewarding, progress throughout the two year course cut some ice with government and an element of coursework was brought in for some subjects, with more introduced over the years. Coursework was also introduced for some A-levels. In practice this meant that each student's standard could be evaluated by producing pieces of work during the course, including essays, projects, case studies, works of art and experiments. These were marked by teachers, with the marks counting towards the final grade. While some subjects remained almost exclusively exam-based, coursework typically accounted for 20-40% of the overall mark. To try to ensure consistency and accuracy, the exam boards checked a sample of the coursework from schools to ensure that teachers weren't being too lenient or too harsh.

Over time, however, the wisdom of coursework was called into question. As the internet plunged headlong into more and more homes, students were, it was said, cutting and pasting whole chunks of other people's work and passing it off as their own. Pushy, ambitious parents assisted their children, and corrupt or fearful teachers helped their pupils to get top marks.

THERE'S SOMETHING ABOUT HARRY

The debate about the pros and cons of coursework really came to a head in 2005, when the third in line to the throne, Prince Harry, was accused of receiving "inappropriate help" from his art teacher while preparing coursework for his AS exam with Edexcel. The allegations were made public when the teacher, Sarah Forsyth, took Eton to an employment tribunal for unfair dismissal – a tribunal that she lost even though she produced a secret tape recording of Prince Harry in an attempt to support her case. She claimed that her head of department ordered her to write five pages of text for the Prince and that she had had finished off one of his paintings for him – claims that were vigorously denied. Even the Royal Family issued a statement denying any cheating.

I was involved in the investigation at the time. We found no evidence to support the claim of cheating, so Prince Harry's grade B stood and the case went away. You should be aware that the numbers of cases involving cheating are comparatively tiny, despite the apparent public concern. Of nearly six million GCSE entries that year, only 1,312 requests for re-moderation were made. The number of actual cases of malpractice involving coursework in GCSE during that summer of 2005 was less than 500. The arguments used to justify the withdrawal of coursework were certainly not based on evidence of actual cheating.

Interestingly, Martin Stephen (him again!), the High Master of top private school, St Paul's, had weighed into the debate a year before the Prince Harry case, when he said: "The internet is a gift to plagiarism. I fully support the move to abolish coursework – it's a government idea that hasn't worked." The High Master's support for the abolitionists' cause was, I'm sure, duly noted, and following the huge amount of media coverage generated by 'Harrygate' the debate about coursework intensified. A review was ordered, which recommended the end of coursework. This decision will have a far reaching impact, but it's too early to say what it will be. I was disappointed with the decision to scrap coursework, since it is very easy to check for plagiarism; the same internet search engines that discover good texts for cheating can also be used to confirm that cheating has taken place.

Since September 2009, coursework for most GCSEs has been replaced by something called controlled assessment. The key thing here is that work done by students during the course still counts. But – and it's a big 'but' – this work, or at least part of it, must be done under 'controlled' conditions. This means supervised by a teacher, rather than done at home. This has caused a lot of problems for anyone taking GCSEs by distance learning as it is just about impossible to administer. See Figure 2 for more on controlled assessment.

Controlled Assessment Explained

Controlled assessment replaced coursework for most GCSEs from 2009 and was introduced for English in 2010 and Science in 2011. Maths has reverted to assessment by exams only. The general rule is that any work that will count towards your final grade must be supervised.

Other 'controls' include time limits and word limits for written work, with the focus on quality, not quantity. If work is completed over several sessions, it will have to be kept in school and can't be taken home.

Controlled assessment identifies three phases of work: task setting, done by the teacher; task taking, done by students; and task marking, done by the teacher, with a sample checked by exam boards.

The table below shows the proportion of controlled assessment for each of the major GCSE subjects. The rest of the marks are based on exam results.

Subject	Proportion of Controlled Assessment
Mathematics	0%
English	60%
Science	25%
History	25%
Geography	25%
ICT	60%
Modern Foreign Languages	25%
Art and Design	60%
Physical Education	60%
Design and Technology	60%
Citizenship	60%
Religious Studies	0%
Business Studies	25%
Applied Subjects: e.g. Manufacturing, Engineering, Health and Social Care, Leisure and Tourism, Applied Business	60%
As you can see from the table, the proportion of controlled assessment varies considerably across subjects, with none at all for Maths, which is entirely based on exams, to 60% for English and applied subjects.	

Figure 2

Girls were always thought to be the hardest working and most conscientious when it came to coursework, and so were the most likely beneficiaries of the old system. As one teacher put it, "you could always tell if it was a girl's course work by the weight of the folder." Time will tell if the new controls help boys to catch up with girls in this important part of the GCSE.

CAN HE DO FLOWER ARRANGING?

What is actually taught, the content of a GCSE, is a constant battle ground, with Royal Societies, university professors, unions (again), teachers, head teachers, authors and many others having a say. The German Ambassador to Britain made headlines a few years back when he wondered out loud why so much emphasis seemed to be on the Nazi period in the A-level history syllabus in the UK. Others, including the present government, want to see much more emphasis on British history, to help imbue a set of shared values and pride in the past. In science, academics bemoan what they consider to be the lack of rigour and Maths content in GCSE Physics and Chemistry, for example. Most of these debates are played out on the pages of national newspapers as well as behind closed doors and around conference room tables. As a student or parent, unless you have a vested interest in any of these debates, my advice would be to wrap your fish and chips up in them and focus on the reality of what is actually in the syllabus of each subject, rather than worry about what the German Ambassador, or anyone else for that matter, thinks.

As well as compulsory subjects, you have a wide choice of optional subjects. Flower arranging isn't currently a

GCSE and despite what you might think by reading the newspapers, it's never likely to be. So who decides what subjects can be taught at GCSE? Ultimately it's the job of the three regulators for England (Ofqual), Wales (DfES) and Northern Ireland (CCEA). They must ensure that standards are maintained over time and decide how GCSEs are structured, assessed and graded. They also dictate how exam boards develop the detail of what will be taught, setting out what students must demonstrate to pass their exams. This is meant to ensure that a GCSE in a subject offered by one exam board is comparable to a GCSE offered by another in the same subject.

You have probably noticed by now that for all of the huffing and puffing about standards, education in the UK heaves with rules, regulations and regulators. Civil servants and consultants pop out of the woodwork to advise, warn and tell teachers, exam boards and others what they can and can't do, what they're doing wrong, what they will do wrong if they continue with a particular course, what they must do instead or why that colour simply doesn't suit them (alright, I made the last one up). You might well wonder 'if only the banking sector had faced such a heavy hand before the credit crunch'. But that of course would just be wishful thinking.

If a new GCSE is to be developed, there needs to be a demand – exam boards sell the courses to schools, and if no-one's going to buy it, no-one's going to develop it. Over the years, new ICT qualifications, a much wider range of languages, reflecting the growing diversity of the UK's population, and new applied GCSEs have been developed and continue to grow. But the number of choices available at GCSE isn't the only thing that's been growing. The last few years have seen a proliferation of alternatives to the GCSE exam and we'll examine these in chapter 4.

THINK AHEAD

One last thing worth mentioning is that when considering what GCSEs to take, it pays to think ahead. If you have plans or ambitions to study at university, you should be aware that your choices and performance at GCSE could be important. With competition for places intense, some universities look at how well students did at GCSE, in addition to A-level, to help them decide whom to admit. Just about every university demands GCSE Maths and English at grade C or above, with some courses looking for at least a B in Maths. Other universities may require a foreign language, whatever subject you want to study there. The 'English Bacc' being pushed by the government may lead more people down a 'traditional' GCSE route, which may or may not suit you. Make sure you keep up to date and be clear about how your GCSE subjects may affect your future.

Chapter 3

THE QUALIFICATIONS: A-LEVEL (OR GCE)

The 'Advanced' or A-level General Certificate of Education (GCE) was introduced in the early 1950s and was the natural progression from the O-level. The A-level became an essential qualification for anyone who wanted to go to university. It has the same function today, but is also a very useful qualification in its own right, opening doors to a number of careers that aren't available to those who just have GCSEs. For this reason, it remains very popular with adult learners as well as teenagers. Many people regard the step up from GCSE to A-level the biggest intellectual leap they ever take.

The first students to take A-level were given only a 'pass' or 'fail', but as more and more people took the exams, the authorities introduced the now famous grades in the 1960s. These were determined by a simple set of rules, which were changed at the start of the 21st Century, leading many of us, including a number of mischievous newspaper reporters, to assume that standards have fallen through the floor. In the old system, students were awarded according to how well they did in relation to all of the other candidates. This was also the way that O-levels were graded, as follows:

A – awarded if you were in the top 10% of all candidates

B – if you were in the next 15% of candidates below an A

C – the next 10% of students below a B

So you can see that the top 35% of all candidates, whatever the total number of marks they were awarded, gained an A, B or C grade.

D – awarded to the 15% of candidates below the C grade

E – given to the 20% of candidates below a D

O – now discarded, this was given to the 20% of candidates beneath an E

Fail (no grade) – given to the bottom 10% of all candidates

The really important aspect of this system was that only 10% of students could gain an 'A', no matter how good the candidates were in any year. At the other end of the scale, 10% would always fail.

This system was modified later to include an 'N' grade to replace the 'O' grade. The 'O' meant that you had achieved O-level standard, but had not done well enough to be awarded an A-level. In case you're wondering, 'N' stood for 'nearly passed'! This grade quickly disappeared for obvious reasons, but it illustrates some of the strange decisions made by civil servants when designing exams.

When A-levels were revised with the introduction of Curriculum 2000 in that year, the method of grading candidates was changed fundamentally. Grades were no longer awarded based on a simple ranking system; instead, exam boards had to assess performance according to a set of complex criteria and award grades based on individual scores. What did this mean in practice? Well, let's say that after looking at the standard of student exams in one subject in a particular year, an exam board decided that a mark of 75% was worth an 'A' grade. *Every student who achieved 75% or more therefore received an 'A'.* Theoretically, if half of all students exceeded 75% they would each get an 'A'. And as things have turned out, it's not uncommon for more than 30% of students to gain an 'A' grade for some subjects in any year.

So, the first lesson on the A-level is that it no longer finds the top and bottom 10%.

You will see from the box that the modern A-level has grown steadily despite a falling birth rate and that success at the top has improved steadily. By 2009 half of the A-levels attempted resulted in a B grade or better. I will have more to say about this trend and the arguments about dumbing down in chapter 8.

A-LEVELS IN THE 21ST CENTURY

Changes to the curriculum in the year 2000 also meant that instead of a single, final exam at the end of two years, the A-level was broken into two separate assessments: the AS-level and the A2. The final A-level grade is calculated after adding up the marks from both, with each part contributing half of the total. Success is no longer based on a single exam. But Curriculum 2000 went further, breaking down the AS and A2 into modules, each of which is assessed separately. The current AS and A2 exams typically have four modules each with the AS set at a lower level of difficulty. Interestingly, the AS is a legitimate stand-alone qualification with its own certificate and has some value, yet the A2 is not separately certificated. The A2 needs to be combined with an AS to create a single A-level.

A-LEVELS IN NUMBERS

1951 – GCE Advanced Levels were introduced for the first time

1963 – Grades were introduced for the first time

2000 – Curriculum 2000 introduced modules, so exams were no longer just taken at the end of the year

2002 – First curriculum 2000: 701,380 entries with 20.7% at grade A and 21.9% at Grade B

2005 – 783,878 entries with 22.8% at grade A and 23.8% at grade B

2009 – 848,977 A2 entries, with 26.7% at grade A and 25.3% at grade B. Including AS and A2, there were more than 2 million entries this year

2011 – 867,317 entries with 8.2% at new A* grade; 18.8% at grade A; and 25.6 at grade B

Source: Joint Council for Qualifications

Students often sit more AS than A2 exams, and the reason is not because they necessarily value an AS, after all it has little recognition in the work-place. Most university places depend upon three appropriate, good A-levels. Students currently tend to go for four or five AS subjects and then drop the subjects in which they perform least well to focus on their three best subjects in the final A2 year; however this practice is under review.

That should be complicated enough, but there's more to confuse.

The A* grade was first awarded in 2010, having been introduced to separate the very best students because so many A grades were being awarded. Fine, but before the A* appeared, a separate, more difficult exam called the Advanced Extension Award (AEA) was introduced to enable very bright students to demonstrate their superiority. The AEA was never popular, was only available in some subjects, and only in some schools and colleges. The trouble is that the AEA still exists (only just), with over 1,500 of them awarded in 2010.

UNDERSTANDING A-LEVEL 'POINTS'

The need to add up the outcomes of the AS and A2 exams created many practical problems. You'd think this would be really easy, but alas it isn't. The administration systems in schools and colleges aren't always great and student transfers add to the risks of error. When you sit an AS exam you have to decide whether you want to 'cash in' the exam result so that it will count towards your final tally of UMS points (see Figure 3). You can 'cash in' before or after you know the results. *However, cash-in administration problems are not uncommon, so be careful.*

UNDERSTAND YOUR UMS FROM YOUR ELBOW

Exam boards need a consistent way of assessing student performance across different exams, marked out of different totals and often taken at different times. It isn't possible to simply use the actual mark attained in the exam, the so-called raw mark. When exam boards decide what grade each mark will receive, they convert the raw mark to a 'uniform mark scale' or UMS. What the examiners in History deem to be worthy of a grade A is given the same UMS mark as what the examiners in Science deem to be worthy of the award of grade A. However, what has been eternally debated is, are the two quantities at the same standard?

The table below shows the minimum UMS mark totals for A-levels, enabling you to add up your UMS marks. You should understand how your UMS total is worked out if you are competing for a university place. The 'units' in the table mean the same as 'modules' – they are the separate parts you study within an AS or A2.

If you had taken a six module (unit) A-level and gained a total of at least 420 UMS points you would gain a grade B: but if you have gained a grade B in a newer four unit A-level you would need at least 280 UMS points. Similarly, to gain a grade C in a two unit A-level you would need at least 120 UMS points.

Admissions teams in top universities often use total UMS point scores to decide who to admit between candidates who gain all As or A*s.

A-level Grade	6 Units Maximum 600 UMS	4 Units Maximum 400 UMS	2 Units Maximum 200 UMS
A*	480 (270 gained at A2)	320 (180 gained at A2)	160 (90 gained at A2)
A	480	320	160
B	420	280	140
C	360	240	120
D	300	200	100
E	240	160	80

Figure 3

Educators and academics are supposed to be clever, but it seems that they are unable to design a clear, transparent system that everyone understands. In fact, the exam system is so complicated that it has enabled the debate about dumbing down to rage on year after year, with both sides unable to show conclusive evidence to prove the claim one way or another. Regretfully, for now, we are stuck with it.

TAKE YOUR PICK

A-levels have plenty of choice, with more than 276 separate exams provided by the different exam boards in subjects ranging from Classical Civilization to Law, and you might be surprised by the number of languages available.

'Applied' A-level variants also exist in some subjects; these tend to feature practical modules and many feature double awards. Double awards are more time consuming and carry double grades, so instead of scoring a single grade B you might score two grade Bs or an A and a B. You can also choose – if your school, college or provider offers it – an 'Extended Project'. The Extended Project and Applied A-levels are assessed differently from standard A-levels, requiring fewer paper exams and more project or practical work.

THE GOLD STANDARD?

A-levels are sometimes referred to as the 'gold standard' of the British educational system, and any attempt to ditch them has always been rejected. You should think of them as having a 'currency' and a 'brand'. If you were to browse through a list of subjects from ten years ago and compare it with the current list, you would notice some differences, particularly in areas such as technology, but the top ten subjects have not changed significantly over that time.

What you study at A-level is critical. The Universities Central Admissions Service (UCAS), and others, have expressed concern about A-level choices. Too many students study subjects that they like, are good at, or that are recommended by others. As always, a good teacher often plays a part in the choice. But too often, students find out later that they cannot gain admission to university because of poor decisions in choosing their subjects. It is sometimes difficult to be certain about future study when starting out with A-level, but you must avoid the risk of turning up with three or four good A-level grades only to be rejected for the particular degree course you want. Universities set out the admission criteria for every degree course, so make sure that you are working towards achievable goals.

One area of controversy is in so-called 'soft' subjects at A-level, with some of the more prestigious universities admitting fewer students with these and more with traditional subjects when compared with their uptake in schools and colleges. The soft options are said to include Media Studies, Law, Art and Design, Photography and Business Studies; less of a gold standard and more of a copper plate, according to the critics. The 'hard' or traditional subjects include pure Sciences, Foreign Languages, History, Geography and English. The Russell Group, which represents 20 of the UK's top universities, has published a list of subjects favoured by admissions tutors and you are likely to be passed over if you take more than one of the out of favour subjects. Studies show that many more students from FE colleges and sixth forms take the so-called soft subjects compared to those attending fee-paying schools. Chapter 5 will help you decide which course or subject is right for you.

As we have seen, A-levels are an important route into higher education, but they do have great value in their own right and are respected across all of industry and commerce and in the civil service. Many excellent careers start with A-levels and despite all that is said about them, the gold standard tag remains and the qualification still carries enormous weight and respect.

Chapter 4

OTHER QUALIFICATIONS: THE GOOD, THE BAD AND THE UGLY

Alongside the well known and well established GCSEs and A-levels, the world of education provides many other qualifications, some of which are so young they can barely stand on their own two feet. If you're after a qualification to be proud of, or are an employer, scratching your head at the weird and wonderful letters after someone's name, it pays to keep up to date with the wide range of awards and qualifications that scramble for attention. Some of them involve exams and some don't, and some are assessed in a variety of different ways.

THE DIPLOMA

This is an important qualification that was introduced in 2008, but it has suffered from over-complex design and bureaucracy. When it was introduced, I warned publicly of the dangers: low attainment rates because of all the hurdles that need to be jumped; an over-complicated administration system, and a grading structure that defies explanation.

These shortcomings are a great shame because employers had high hopes for it and some teachers did, too.

However, its future looks bleak and some exam boards have decided to stop offering the Diploma as a whole. Nevertheless, the majority of universities recognise it as a valid admission qualification. The present government seems more interested in a Baccalaureate for England (the Welsh already have one) and it seems that the Diploma is falling from favour as the English Baccalaureate takes priority.

The Diploma is offered in 14 'lines of learning' but these are being reduced. Typically, schools, colleges and employers all contribute different parts of the qualification. It is supposed to offer hands-on, practical experience, as well as classroom learning, with the accent on the world of work. It comes in three flavours:

- ✓ Foundation Diploma – equivalent to five GCSEs at grades D to G

- ✓ Higher Diploma – equivalent to seven GCSEs at grades A* to C

- ✓ Advanced Diploma – equivalent to three and a half A-levels.

For those aged over 16, there's another version called a Progression Diploma, which is effectively a part-completion of an Advanced Diploma. You might call it an 'almost Diploma'. It was probably introduced because the full Diploma is so difficult to gain. You might think this is crazy, and I might agree.

Each Diploma, whatever the level, has three major areas of study.

1. **Principal Learning** – compulsory and focused on the chosen subject (known as the 'line of learning'). It contributes half of the total award and consists of a series of modules.

2. **Generic Learning** – common to all Diplomas, whatever the subject. It includes Functional Skills assessments in English, Maths and ICT (with complicated rules about levels) plus Personal Learning and Thinking Skills (PLTS). A Project and at least ten days work experience also feature.

3. **Additional and Specialist Learning** – this tops up the Diploma – and rather confusingly consists of other stand-alone qualifications, such as GCSEs or vocational courses.

The Diploma is very difficult to achieve, demanding two years of study and success in each separate element. A total of 10,241 Diplomas were awarded in 2011, more than doubling the previous year. Higher Diplomas, equivalent to good GCSE passes, dominated the numbers. Success rates are poor. When Diploma results are published you might spot a very careful use of language. Statistics are provided for the number of Diplomas *completed*, but there are no statistics for the number of Diplomas *attempted*.

Think carefully before choosing a Diploma. It was the flagship of the previous government and was given massive publicity and support, even incurring the wrath of the Advertising Standards Authority for one of its adverts. The government is much less enthusiastic and has announced that it is to close the Diploma Aggregation Service from 2013; this is the system used to bring together the different components needed to gain the whole qualification, although Principal Learning and the Project will still be available as independent qualifications. If you intend to study for an Advanced Diploma in order to win a university place, check the appropriate levels closely and make sure that the universities you are interested in accept it. Most students have stuck with the A-level.

Functional Skills

These are new qualifications in their own right, which were launched in 2010, although they were trialled for three years before that. Functional Skills provide training in Maths, English and ICT (Information and Communications Technology) in a practical context. They were supposed to become a compulsory element of GCSEs to address the concerns of employers that school leavers had poor literacy and numeracy. But students performed badly during the trials and so the notion of compulsory Functional Skills in GCSE was abandoned. Interestingly, they are still compulsory as part of the Diploma and contribute significantly to poor Diploma completion rates. Expect to see Functional Skills appear in apprenticeship programmes in the future.

INTERNATIONAL GCSEs (IGCSE)

IGCSEs are an international version of GCSE exams, with hundreds of thousands of students in more than 100 countries taking them each year. They were developed originally by the University of Cambridge Local Examinations Syndicate (UCLES, now Cambridge Assessment) but are now offered by other exam boards. Like GCSEs they have foundation and higher tiers and are graded from A* to G, but unlike GCSEs they don't usually include any coursework or controlled assessment, and are tested by written exams at the end of the course.

For many years these qualifications were not funded by the government in UK state schools, but that is changing and the government has lifted the restriction from these being taught in comprehensives and academies. IGCSEs have long been popular in fee-paying schools, which seem to like the traditional forms of assessment, a bit like the O-levels of old. They're also proving a hit with distance learning providers, for whom the need to manage controlled assessment tasks has often proven to be one administrative hurdle too far; things are much simpler with end of year exams. IGCSEs do provide a grade-for-grade equivalent to GCSEs, so employers can be sure of their quality; they also allow progression to more advanced study, such as A-levels, and are recognised by universities.

VOCATIONAL QUALIFICATIONS

Vocational qualifications cover a multitude of work- related disciplines and are available at all levels – from pre-GCSE to postgraduate. You can do a vocational qualification at school or college, or as part of an apprenticeship. You can also study for one by distance learning, or at work. Your performance in a vocational course will be judged by some form of continuous assessment, rather than a written exam, which appeals to many people.

Choosing a vocational subject tends to be easier than choosing a GCSE or A-level because most people do so with a particular job or career in mind. The range is vast - from Accident Repair and Bricklaying to Visual Merchandising and Veterinary Practice - and several different organisations may offer similar courses. In an attempt to help people understand different vocational qualifications, the regulator created the Qualifications and Credit Framework (QCF) – see chapter 1. Unfortunately, the QCF is too complicated. It cost a great deal of money to develop, describes eight different levels of difficulty and tabulates all units in all qualifications against a scale. It's a bureaucrat's dream, disliked by exam boards and many education providers, who have had to spend a great deal of time and money restructuring their qualifications to fit the new framework. It's of little use to teachers and the current government has displayed no enthusiasm for the project.

More than 100 organisations offer vocational qualifications and the range of qualifications offered grows each year as new skills and careers evolve. Several national awarding organisations, such as City & Guilds, offer a huge range of management and supervisory qualifications, for example. The rest of this section takes you through some of the most common vocational qualifications you may encounter.

NVQs (NATIONAL VOCATIONAL QUALIFICATIONS)

These are widely used throughout the country and are delivered in the workplace. They exist in many forms and at different levels, from level 1 (pre-GCSE) to level 5 (equivalent to a Foundation Degree). Each one is sector and task specific. NVQs are outcome based rather than examined and are commonly delivered directly by employers or specialist training providers. Anyone taking an NVQ is usually assessed on a portfolio of evidence and practical assignments. It's unusual for schoolchildren to 'take' an NVQ, although they are a key part of apprenticeships, which are available for those aged 16 and over. Achieving an NVQ demonstrates practical skill and ability in a particular sector, such as Construction, Planning and the Built Environment, or Agriculture, Horticulture and Animal Care.

BTECs

This is a group of qualifications that has existed for more than 25 years. Primarily aimed at providing workplace skills, they also enable progression to further and higher education; more than 60,000 BTEC students routinely go on to take a degree each year. BTECs have a very strong brand and recognition throughout industry and commerce, appearing at every level of ability. You will find Entry, Introductory, Nationals, Higher Nationals, and a range of professional development short courses. BTECs are commonly taught in further education colleges, but have grown popular in schools in recent years. BTECs are not externally examined in the same way as GCSEs and

A-levels. Instead they are assessed by teachers and samples of student work are submitted to exam boards for checking (or moderation, to give it its official title). This is based on practical work and portfolios. However, the company that provides the qualification, Pearson, has announced that the next generation of BTECs will include an element of external assessment from September 2012.

In recent years BTEC Firsts have gained 'GCSE- equivalent' status and been taken up by more and more schools. This means that they count towards the crucial league tables. Schools offering these qualifications have found that the assessment and learning style works very well with many students, particularly those who enjoy learning by doing. All well and good, you might think, but in our education system, things are rarely as straightforward as they seem. Because achievement rates are higher in BTEC Firsts than GCSEs, some teachers have been accused of trying to boost league table results. The current government has warned that it will revise the rules to prevent GCSE-equivalent qualifications from boosting league table points.

Nevertheless, BTECs and equivalent City & Guilds and OCR qualifications will continue because of employer demand and remain the strongest brand in vocational or applied learning. City & Guilds is a very well known and respected awarding body specialising in vocational qualifications. They are certainly a viable alternative to traditional academic teaching and assessment, providing a route to higher education from the age of 14.

BACCALAUREATES

These are programmes of study and qualifications that aim to give a rounded education and are typically applied from pre-primary to age 19. Perhaps the most well-known is the International Baccalaureate, or IB. At higher levels, it is characterised by far less specialisation than A-levels, with students typically studying Science, Humanities, Arts and Languages as part of the package. It has found favour in many private schools, which don't follow the national curriculum. However, it is expensive to deliver compared with the national system and the number of people taking it is comparatively tiny in the UK, although it is growing. With globalisation the IB may become a major qualification in the future since it is one of the few truly international qualifications. The IB is part of UNESCO and based in Switzerland, with assessment centres in many countries.

The popularity of the IB has given rise to clones, and there is a Welsh Baccalaureate. More recently one of the major exam boards, AQA, has developed its own version – the AQA-BAC – again taken up in tiny numbers. The English Baccalaureate (or 'English Bacc') is currently underway but it could be different from the IB in many ways. It might not ultimately be a qualification that leads to a certificate, but simply a list of subjects that can gain league table points for schools. The initial proposal was for this English version to include Mathematics, English, Science, History or Geography and a Modern Foreign Language. Critics suggest that the English Bacc is little more than tinkering with league tables, which would be ironic, given the government's criticism of such steps in opposition.

But whatever you think of the English Bacc – and opinions are mixed – it has definitely roared up the government's education agenda, leaving qualifications like the Diploma trailing in its wake. Some teachers believe it will steer pupils down a narrow academic path that may not suit them, while others think it will lead to greater academic rigour and boost standards.

THE CAMBRIDGE PRE-U

This is an interesting initiative launched in 2008 by Cambridge Assessment to address concerns that A-levels were no longer rigorous enough or able to differentiate the best students. Such concern came mainly from fee-paying schools. As its name implies, the Pre-U is designed to act as a substitute for A-levels to aid university admission decisions. It has been taken up by a number of 'top' schools, but again, in insignificant numbers.

PROFESSIONAL QUALIFICATIONS

Many adults combine work and study to enhance their skills and knowledge and develop their careers. While many part-time students study academic and vocational qualifications, some also study for professional qualifications, which are accredited by the relevant professional body. These qualifications – and what is learnt by studying them - don't only look good on your *Curriculum Vitae* (CV), but provide real world skills and knowledge that can be put to practical use immediately. Many professional associations have sophisticated qualifications and assessment operations, developing the syllabus, setting and marking exams and coursework, and awarding candidates with certificates – and in some cases, letters after their names. This helps to ensure that a level of professional competence is maintained by membership of the relevant organisation.

Distance learning providers offer a large number of professional qualifications, giving support and back-up that many people find useful. Such qualifications are usually available at several different levels, depending on current knowledge, skill and experience. Organisations that provide office-related qualifications include the Chartered Institute of Personnel and Development (CIPD); the Chartered Institute of Management Accountants (CIMA); the Chartered Institute of Marketing (CIM) and the International Association of Book-keepers (IAB). Lots of other professional organisations provide qualifications in specific fields, such as Health or IT – Microsoft, for example, has a very wide range of certificates in areas such as Security, Programming and Systems Architecture. If you want to advance your career – or enter into a profession you're not yet involved in – then take a look at what professional qualifications are out there.

Chapter 5

WHICH SUBJECTS SHOULD YOU CHOOSE?

C an you have too much choice? Whether you choose GCSE, A-level, vocational or professional courses, you can bet that the options available will outstrip the choice of toothpaste at your local supermarket. At GCSE, Maths, English and Science are compulsory, but after that the choice is vast (see Figure 6). For example, exam boards currently offer about 70 different GCSE subjects. One thing to keep an eye on is whether government whims may make other subjects compulsory in the future. For instance, the 'English Baccalaureate', a new GCSE performance measure, may lead to growing numbers of students choosing a foreign language as this is one of the subjects you will have to take in order to achieve it. Foreign Languages fuelled many heated debates when they were taken off the 'compulsory' list a few years back, but the 'English Bacc' may persuade many schools to insist that their students take a language from now on. See Figure 4 for what's compulsory and what's not.

If you're an adult learner, you can choose whatever GCSE subjects interest you the most. All A-level subjects are optional, whatever your age, and the choice of vocational

WHAT'S COMPULSORY AND WHAT'S NOT FOR GCSE?

The current compulsory subjects at GCSE for school children are Mathematics, English and Science. Schools must then offer *at least one* subject from the following categories:

- ✓ Modern foreign languages – such as French, German or Spanish
- ✓ Humanities - such as History and Geography
- ✓ Design and technology
- ✓ Arts – such as Music, Dance, Drama and Art

Depending on the school, other choices are likely to include some of the following, although the exact course names may vary:

- ✓ Business studies
- ✓ Engineering
- ✓ Health and social care
- ✓ Leisure and tourism
- ✓ Manufacturing
- ✓ Social sciences

The government insists that schools teach a number of other areas, although these don't always lead to a qualification. They include Citizenship, Careers Education, ICT, Physical Education, Religious Studies, Sex and Relationships Education and some kind of Work Related Learning.

Figure 4

and professional qualifications at all levels is vast. Think of any sector in the economy and the chances are that you'll find a qualification for it.

Schools, colleges and training providers decide what exam subjects and other courses to offer according to the interests and expertise of their teachers, their equipment and facilities, the budget, student demand and the support provided by the exam boards. See Figure 5 for the ten most popular GCSE and A-level subjects in 2011.

The ten most popular exam subjects in 2011	
GCSE	**A-level**
1. Mathematics	1. English
2. English	2. Mathematics
3. English Literature	3. Biology
4. Science	4. Psychology
5. Additional Science	5. History
6. Design and Technology	6. Chemistry
7. Religious Studies	7. Art and Design
8. History	8. General Studies
9. Art and Design	9. Media/Film/TV Studies
10. Geography	10. Physics

Figure 5 Source: Joint Council for Qualifications

At GCSE, more than three quarters of a million students took Maths in 2011, and the separate sciences were up again on the previous year, continuing to gain in popularity.

Interestingly, girls are moving to these subjects quicker than boys. French was down again, this time by over 13%, and German fell by the same amount, reflecting the impression that students who take languages tend to have natural skills; everyone else thinks it's a hard option. At A-level, Maths continued to increase in popularity with the Sciences again showing increases. These choices show an increasing trend towards the 'harder' subjects, perhaps reflecting university admission demands and the increased interest in new technologies.

What If The Subject You Want To Study Isn't Offered?

If a learning provider, school or college doesn't offer the subject that you are particularly interested in, there is very little you can do about it. Parents should have started a conversation about the school introducing the course as soon as their children joined in year 7; now in year 9 it's probably too late. You can, however, enter your son or daughter as a private candidate, and the school may even pay the exam fees and invigilate during the exams, but you should think carefully about the time, effort and sacrifice this will entail. It's probably most common in foreign languages, where a child brought up with one or two non-native English speakers studies Chinese, Italian, Arabic or another language outside of school and takes it as an additional exam at the end of the year.

If the school doesn't offer Engineering and your heart is set on it, you'll face great practical difficulties in completing the practical work required. By all means talk it through with the head teacher, but you'll probably find that a good grounding in Maths and Science subjects will stand you in good stead for the future. But while your school or college won't offer every subject available, even the smallest school now offers a much wider choice of subjects compared with 10 or 15 years ago. If you're an adult learner, you should check what's offered by local colleges and distance learning providers to find the course you want. You'll often be able to join a distance learning course at any time of the year. With a college, you'll have to fit in with their term times. But what subject will maximise your chances of success, help your future career and ensure that you're not bored stiff ?

Too Much Choice – or Not Enough?

If you want to – or have to – study GCSE, on the face of it you have a very big choice; see the list of the main GCSE optional subject areas (Figure 6). Each of these subjects demands different skills and capabilities. If you're at school, after the compulsory subjects (see Figure 4), you may have four or five options to choose if you take the 'average' of nine GCSEs, including Maths, English and Science. But bear in mind that some schools insist on students taking certain subjects in addition to these, which can considerably reduce the amount of choice. For example, some schools with a religious ethos insist on their students taking a GCSE in Religious Studies, whilst others require their brighter students to take a language and many now make Physical Education a compulsory GCSE. The 'English Bacc' may lead to more schools insisting on their students taking History or Geography, as well as a Foreign Language. The options available in some schools are much narrower in practice than the number of potential GCSE choices would suggest. Schools usually make students choose their options in February of year 9, so you should ensure that you have as much information as possible about what's on offer. See Figure 6 for the main optional subjects at GCSE.

The main optional subjects at GCSE	
• Art and Design	• History
• Business and Communication Systems	• Home Economics
• Business Studies	• Information and Communication Technology (ICT)
• Citizenship Studies	• Law
• Classical Civilization	• Leisure and Tourism
• Dance	• Manufacturing
• Design and Technology	• Media Studies
• Drama	• Other foreign languages
• Economics	• Music
• Engineering	• Physical Education (PE)
• French	• Psychology
• Geography	• Religious Studies
• German	• Sociology
	• Spanish

Figure 6

HELPING YOU TO DECIDE

When thinking about your choice of what subject to take, you should ask yourself a few questions.

WHAT DO YOU WANT TO DO NEXT?

If you have an idea about a particular career, or going to university, you should bear this in mind when choosing your GCSE options, even though you haven't even started them yet. Here's some food for thought.

- ✓ Some universities may consider GCSE (or equivalent) grades when offering places on competitive degree courses. If you get more than a couple of grade Ds at GCSE, you may not get in – so it pays now to choose subjects that give you the most chance of success.

- ✓ All universities require a minimum of grade C at Maths and English at GCSE for any degree course – and some courses, such as Business degrees, may insist on a B, or even an A.

- ✓ Some careers demand specific qualifications. If you want to be a vet, you'll need grade As in Science A-levels (or equivalent), so you should do as much science as you can at GCSE. If you want to be an engineer, good grades in Maths and Science will be crucial – although a vocational course may be a great option for you, in which case you won't have to take exams.

Bear in mind, though, that for many careers, GCSE options are less important than what comes next. If you want to be a lawyer or barrister, GCSE Law is not compulsory – and neither, interestingly enough, is A-level Law. In fact, several eminent institutions seem to actively discourage it, regarding it as one of the soft A-levels. A good grounding in subjects that require you to write well, express yourself clearly and argue a case from evidence are likely to be just as helpful, such as English, History or Economics. In general, however, if you intend to progress further up the qualifications ladder, it makes sense to study the same subjects, or at least some of them, at a lower level first.

WHAT ARE YOU GOOD AT?

You should seriously consider choosing options that you have done well in so far. If you are good at languages, do a language; if you enjoy writing, subjects like History and Geography will give you the chance to shine; if you're good at Maths, maybe an extra science subject or a course like Economics, if it's offered, will suit you.

If you were good at a particular subject during years 7, 8 and 9, or back in the day when you were at school, then the chances are you'll continue to be good at it. Good grades throughout the early years of school are the most reliable indicator of future success, and while there are no guarantees, choosing an option in which you already have a track record will stand you in very good stead.

What if you're really good at a subject, but can't stand it? This does happen occasionally and can be frustrating for parents, teachers and students alike. If you're a parent, negotiate; could your child put up with it for a couple of years, sure in the knowledge that they're likely to get a high grade at GCSE and can then drop it and never let it darken their timetable again? With several options to play with, it's a shame to lose what appears to be a 'banker' without a very good alternative. However, if their hatred of the subject, or of the teacher that will be teaching it, is so intense, then it may be best to drop it as the presumed good grades may never materialise.

WHAT INTERESTS AND MOTIVATES YOU?

Most students take their GCSE, A-level or vocational courses over two years, so a key factor for many people – teenagers in particular – is trying to beat the boredom. If you're interested in something, study a subject that comes close and will give you some insights into it. This will maximise your chance of success. Adult students often have motivation in spades, considering the sacrifice that many make to re-enter the world of education. Well motivated students are a teacher's or lecturer's dream; there's more chance they'll succeed and more chance they'll do the work that will help them – it's a virtuous circle.

WHAT ARE YOU LIKE?

If you're at school or college, knowing what makes you tick can help you to make the right choice. Listen to your teachers and lecturers – they'll know your strengths and weakness and will often compete for the best students. If you're a practical person; or creative, sociable or curious, think about which subjects might suit you the best. Art, Music and Drama may seem obvious choices for a creative person, but perhaps that creativity could be put to good use in a Business course.

How do you like to learn?

Practical people often like a hands-on, learning by doing approach, but that isn't for everyone. Some people like reading, studying and note taking; others prefer listening, watching and talking things through. So when you are deciding what to study, consider how you like to learn. Take into account the emphasis that each course places on your preferred learning style.

How do you feel about exams?

Another factor to take into account is how you feel about taking exams. For some students it's a white knuckle ride that quite literally makes them break out in a sweat; for others it's a bit like riding a bike. If you are in the former category, find out how much of the final mark will be based on end of year exams and how much on some form of controlled assessment. Choosing a subject with more controlled assessment and fewer exams may make the difference between success and failure or a top grade and an average one. Remember that BTECs and other vocational courses currently have no exams at all and many professional qualifications are assessed on coursework or a portfolio of work and evidence.

GET AS MUCH HELP AS YOU CAN

Whether you know what you want to do with your education or not, it makes sense to get as much advice as possible about what will help. In the past, you could be pretty sure that your school or college would have a careers adviser to help you make the right decisions. But as austerity measures bite and local councils are forced to make savings, you may find that this is no longer the case. Web-based and telephone advice will be available, but it seems certain that face-to-face guidance will be cut back. Schools will have to find the money to fund careers advice out of their own coffers, so it won't be guaranteed. Under these circumstances, you should do as much as you can to ensure you're well informed. Check out *www.examlinks.co.uk* for pointers and sources of further information.

KEEPING IT IN THE FAMILY

Is there someone in the family with something useful to say about career options, or a particular subject? Maybe there's an aunt or uncle, a cousin, or a cousin's friend, who has some useful information. People use these networks all the time in the workplace; websites such as *Linked In* (*www.linkedin.com*) exist to support it, so why shouldn't you link in to people you know? Later on, these contacts may prove useful if you need some work experience, which is a requirement for all pupils in years 10 and 11.

Whilst careers advice and guidance might be cut, most schools, colleges and learning providers are good at providing information about the choices available, so make sure you use them. Read the pamphlet, attend the options evening, speak to teachers. Teachers are particularly important; they do compete for bright, motivated students, and you should be flattered if they seem to be competing over you. But above all, they should give you an honest appraisal of your strengths and weaknesses and a realistic assessment of how you're likely to do if you choose a particular course or subject. Some schools and colleges offer taster sessions in new subjects, which are worth trying.

WHAT TO AVOID

Just as there are many factors to take into account when choosing what subject or subjects to study, it's also worth avoiding a few things.

IT'S NOT A MAN'S WORLD

For school children in particular, parents should convey the message that there are no girls' or boys' subjects – just subjects. The statistics indicate that some subjects are more popular among one or other of the sexes, but this shouldn't be the deciding factor. Of course, if you have a daughter who wants to study an Applied GCSE in Construction, the fact that the rest of the class consists of 25 boys may put her off. That's understandable, but you – and the school – should support her if that's what she really wants to do.

HIS (OR HER) BEST MATE'S DOING IT

Peer pressure is an irresistible force in the lives of many teenagers. If you're a parent, try to persuade your son or daughter that it shouldn't be the deciding factor when choosing what GCSEs to study for the next two years. If they let others decide what courses to follow, the chances are that they'll end up doing options that suit their friends better than them. While having friends doing the same course can be a great help, it can also be a distraction if your child isn't really interested in it.

HER (OR HIS) FAVOURITE TEACHER

Sometimes students make decisions based on their like or dislike of certain teachers. But of course, there's no guarantee that the teacher they like will actually take them for the subject when they move onto their GCSEs, nor that the teacher will still be at the school for the next two years. Nevertheless, the relationship with a teacher is an important one, and decisions based on it can be rational, not just emotional. The best advice is probably to make this a factor in any decision, but not the clincher; after all, if you really love a subject, you can probably get over the fact that you don't love the teacher quite so much.

THE LAST MINUTE RUSH

Year 9 pupils know that their options are coming and that they'll need to make a decision by the end of the second term. So there's no reason to select their options in a rush and then claim they didn't have enough time. Parents can help by talking things through in good time to avoid the last minute rush. Adult learners have no such problem.

OPTIONS CHECKLIST

Things to bear in mind when choosing what subjects to study

- ✓ Are you interested in the subject?

- ✓ Are you any good at the subject – or in something similar?

- ✓ Is the subject something you might want to study at a higher level?

- ✓ Does the subject suit your career aspirations?

- ✓ Does it suit the type of person you are?

- ✓ Will it help you to use your preferred learning style?

- ✓ Do you like the teacher?

- ✓ Does the subject have the right mix of exams and assessment?

COPING WITH DISAPPOINTMENT

One thing to bear in mind when choosing options at school is that you may not be able to do all of the options you choose. Some subjects may be oversubscribed, while others may be dropped because of a lack of interest. Some compromise may be required – you may get X, but not Y because of a timetable clash. Schools do their best to ensure that pupils can do the subjects they want, but it's not always possible. Parents can help children get over this disappointment. For 14 year olds in particular, the GCSE or equivalent subjects that you end up doing probably won't make or break your future career, and while failure to get exactly what you want can be horrendous at the time, you'll get over it.

CHOOSING HIGHER LEVEL COURSES

The 2011 summer exams featured about 70 different A-levels in a wide range of subjects, from Critical Thinking to Welsh Language. Like GCSE, A-levels come in a variety of sizes and shapes: A-level; Applied A-level double award; Applied A-level single award. BTEC National awards, which are equivalent to A-level, also come in great varieties. So how do you choose?

If you intend to go on to university or some form of higher education, the right place to start is at the end. A-levels and their equivalents are the key to university admission. Universities list the minimum admission requirements for each course of study, so read them carefully, remembering that for oversubscribed courses, you might need to do better than the minimum. Too many students choose

A-level subjects for the wrong reasons, such as liking the subject or staying with classmates. There's nothing wrong with liking the subject, but if it's unrelated to the kind of degree you want to study, you should think again. Understand the subject, the UMS marks needed for the grade and the number of different A-levels that you will need and base your choices on that understanding. Spend some time looking through the admissions requirements for a few universities. You will see many different types of qualifications listed, but look closely at the A-levels. Do you need an A or a B? Notice how often English and Maths appear. English and Maths, which are compulsory at GCSE, are really important subjects and you should think carefully before avoiding them.

TOO SOFT TO HANDLE?

Bear in mind the controversy around so-called 'soft' A-level subjects. There's evidence that some elite institutions reject some 'non-preferred' subjects on the grounds that they're not rigorous enough. If you take too many of these and plan to apply to a 'Russell Group' university to study, you may be disappointed (the Russell Group represents 20 of the UK's top universities).

One study found that in 2007-08, Oxford University accepted more students with Further Mathematics A-level than students with the following A-levels combined: Accounting, Art and Design, Business Studies, Communication Studies, Design and Technology, Drama/Theatre Studies, Film Studies, Home Economics, ICT,

Law, Media Studies, Music Technology, Psychology, Sports Studies/Physical Education, and Travel and Tourism. Many more state school and college students take these latter subjects than students at fee paying schools. But whatever you think of the rights and wrongs of this, you need to get the facts about current entry requirements to avoid disappointment.

ARE APPLIED A-LEVELS FOR YOU?

Applied A-levels represent a very small proportion of the total number of A-level awards. In 2011 there were more than 850,000 entries for the traditional A-level and just over 42,000 entries for double and single award Applied A-levels (down on the previous year). As with the GCSE, Applied A-levels feature fewer written exams so they are worth considering if you prefer to be assessed by some form of practical work.

There are no easy options. If you look at the results the Applied A-level is no push over. In 2011 about 27% of traditional A-levels were awarded at grades A* and A, but in the same year just 7.4% of Applied A-levels were awarded these grades.

Source: Joint Council for Qualifications

PLAN ALTERNATIVES

When you study A-levels as a route to university, as a teenager or as an adult, it can seem as though your whole future depends on a single summer of exams, and the world appears black and white. Plan for a range of outcomes and be sure that you have an alternative when your trembling hands open up the results envelope. Thinking ahead, the Sciences will become critically important for careers and for the economy as a whole. The government is putting a great deal of emphasis and funding into the so-called STEM subjects – Science, Technology, Engineering and Mathematics. At an early stage in school you can afford to choose some subjects based on their attraction. As you progress and your career ambitions develop you should increasingly focus on the skills and qualifications that you will need. Try to think about a sort of converging path in your studies.

A-LEVELS AND CAREERS

Whilst A-levels are often crucial for entry to higher education, many people end their education with them and do very well. A-levels can be a way into careers that are beyond those who just have GCSEs, with some firms taking on successful A-level students in fields as diverse as engineering, accountancy and computing. As you progress to more advanced areas of study you should think carefully about your own personal goals and ambitions, and how education and qualifications can help. A-levels can boost your job prospects, help you enter a profession or move you into a new field. For some people, the intellectual challenge is enough, as is the satisfaction of gaining a valuable qualification that is still highly regarded.

A-levels can open up opportunities across a wide range of careers. Consulting organisations such as KPMG look for good A-level students. Many of the professions including law and chartered accountancy welcome A-level entrants. Healthcare offers many routes. The civil service and armed forces take in thousands of A-level entrants each year. If you are a student, check whether your school or college is a member of U-Explore, the careers, information and guidance service (see *www.u-explore.com*). Their resources are staggering and cover virtually every job that you can imagine. Alternatively, take a few minutes to browse through one of the major online job vacancy boards such as Jobsite or Monster and see how many opportunities depend on A-levels. More than ever, A-levels can provide the entry to a job where further personal development and training are provided.

Chapter 6

HOW TO ACHIEVE BETTER RESULTS

I f you're studying for a qualification or exam, you should be trying to obtain the best results you can. Better results will help you to do the more advanced course you're interested in, help you get into the university you want and look better on your CV. Whatever your motivation, better is best. For many of us, though, we try for a better mark more out of hope than expectation. We hope we get lucky with the exam questions; hope that we've revised the right bits of the syllabus, and hope that the examiner is in a good mood when he or she looks at our work. Often we feel we can't quite cut it, that we don't have enough ability or skill, or that we're simply not bright enough. When you're up late studying or revising and the topic is still not sinking in, you can be forgiven for thinking that the media hype about falling standards and trained monkeys being able to pass exams is all rubbish.

But while ability, skill, intelligence and luck all play a part in exam success, you can take steps to improve your chances. By following the advice given here, you're not going to leap from a grade D to a grade A overnight. But you could go from a D to a C, which is regarded as a good pass and is all that many employers look for when considering job applications. Or perhaps your predicted B grade could become an A, ensuring you get into the university you'd set your heart on.

In this chapter we'll look at how you can achieve better results by studying more effectively, coping better with revision and exams and understanding the many ways of giving yourself an advantage to lift your grades.

LUCKY FOR SOME – 13 LESSONS TO HELP YOU GAIN BETTER GRADES

LESSON 1: USE THE HELP AVAILABLE

Let's start with the most fundamental thing – learning the information and developing the skills you need to pass whatever it is you're studying. Whether you're taking an academic course, a professional qualification or a vocational award with no exams, you should use all of the help and advice on offer from your school, college, provider or professional association. Such help may include catch up sessions, clubs in different subjects or specially produced study guides. Not everyone makes the most of these opportunities to achieve better results, so make sure you do.

LESSON 2: DON'T RESIGN YOURSELF TO DOING BADLY

It's strange that as schools and colleges have become better at teaching their students how to answer exam questions, study skills aren't usually given the same priority. In fact, some universities find that even after A-levels, a number of students struggle with the demands of higher education and run study skills sessions to help them cope. A good teacher or tutor is worth his or her weight in gold in this respect, as they can give you advice and feedback throughout the year. Many schools provide homework books and ask parents to sign them each week; whether or not your school does this, you or your son or daughter should keep on top of the workload and course requirements.

If you are struggling in a subject, speak about it with the relevant teacher or tutor – don't keep silent and resign yourself to doing badly.

Another way younger students in particular may resign themselves to doing badly is estimated or predicted grades. For more than 20 years, children at the end of primary school have taken national curriculum tests and been awarded a 'level' for each subject. The government's target has been for children to achieve a level 4 in English and Maths, although not all achieve it. When these children enter secondary school, they often find that they are streamed in certain subjects according to how well they did in these tests, along with a teacher assessment of their abilities. Levels are often sub-divided, so a 4a is better than a 4b for instance. If you're considered a 4a student, the chances are that your target will be a 6a by the time you get to the end of year 9. Your level at the end of year 9 will then determine your estimated GCSE grades. While this may seem sensible, it can also become a self-fulfilling prophecy: you expect to reach a certain level, and your teachers do too. But why be limited? Don't let these expectations, derived from your performance as an 11-year-old, dictate your performance.

People grow, learn and improve, so don't rely too much on these estimates, because that's all they are. You can do better.

LESSON 3: YOU DON'T NEED TO KNOW EVERYTHING TO DO WELL

Some people will inevitably struggle with some subjects, but there may be some parts of it that they can understand better than others. In Maths, for example, perhaps they don't get algebra, but can understand shapes and geometry. By focusing on their strengths, they're unlikely to get an A grade, but may learn enough about some parts of the syllabus to obtain a grade C, which is recognised as a good pass. You don't need to know the whole syllabus equally well to obtain a good result, whatever you're studying.

LESSON 4: KEEP ORGANISED

If you're at school or college, you may well be studying lots of subjects at the same time. If you're an adult learner, you've probably got the day job to worry about and are juggling lots of different commitments. Whatever your circumstances, to get a good result you need to keep on top of things. Keeping files or folders for different subjects will help, so long as they are easy to use. Part of being organised is planning what you're going to do and when, so allow enough time to do all of the work that's required. This matters if you're preparing for exams or controlled assessments, or are doing a vocational course and need to keep a file of work as evidence of your ability.

LESSON 5: *GET A COPY OF THE INSTRUCTIONS*
GIVEN TO EXAMINERS

When exam papers are designed, exam boards always produce a companion document called a Mark Scheme. This gives instructions to examiners on how marks are to be allocated to each question and how to make judgments. It's the most important document when markers are trained how to mark each exam paper. Some marks are only awarded if students give specific responses, but others allow examiner discretion. Mark schemes are incredibly useful because they show exactly how to win marks, so consider using them throughout your course, not just when preparing for exams and tackling past papers. Mark schemes are usually available free of charge from exam board websites. Download last year's question paper and its companion mark scheme and check how the marks were allocated. You will also see what questions carried the most marks and this will help you to plan. If you can't get the mark scheme directly, ask your school, college or learning provider.

LESSON 6: *ACT ON PROBLEMS*

Sometimes your teacher, lecturer or tutor can be a problem. If you don't like him (or her) it can become an insurmountable barrier. Sometimes, particularly at school, children may be taught the same subject by several teachers, which some find disruptive. Sometimes a teacher may be on long term sick leave and that subject is then taught by a succession of supply teachers, which can also disrupt continuity and hold back progress. If you have concerns about any of these issues, discuss them with the school or college. If schools and colleges have been sticking to the syllabus, this can be less of a problem than you might think, but speak up if you have any concerns.

LESSON 7: USE STUDY GUIDES

Study guides exist for most subjects, providing insights into the key aspects of the syllabus and hints and tips on answering exam questions. They can be pricey, but if you can afford it, then buying one for the subject or subjects you struggle with could be a good investment. Many schools and colleges will loan them to students or sell them at a discount and they are often available in public libraries. You should check that the guide you buy or borrow is relevant. For example, some History GCSEs cover modern world history (basically the 20th century), while others cover earlier periods, so make sure you get the right one. Of course once you've obtained the guide, you have to do something with it. Spending a short period of time, say half an hour a day, on different sections is a good idea. Breaking study time up into small, manageable chunks over a long period of time is often more effective and less daunting than spending hours on end poring over books just before the day of the exam.

LESSON 8: HIRE A PRIVATE TUTOR

A private tutor is the most expensive option of the lot. Depending on where in the country you live, you can expect to pay anything from £20 upwards per hour. For many people, this is not a realistic option, but if you can afford it, then a tutor could be a big help to you, or your son or daughter in a particular subject for a couple of reasons.

Firstly, for children still at school, the tutor is not one of their teachers. This will immediately give them brownie points.

Secondly, they provide intensive, one-to-one support, guiding you through those parts of the syllabus you struggle with. They can pinpoint where you've been going wrong, explain ways of doing it (whatever 'it' is) and guide you through worked examples and questions, increasing your confidence and ability.

However, employing a private tutor is no guarantee of success. How do you know if the tutor knows his or her stuff? How can you check? The best way of employing a tutor, like a plumber or builder, is through a personal recommendation from someone you trust. But if you're like most people, you won't know anyone that's employed a tutor, so here are a few tips to bear in mind before you decide to take one on.

- ✓ Ask for references – and be sure to check them.
- ✓ Ask for information about their teaching experience – and check that out, too.
- ✓ Find out how long they have been tutoring.
- ✓ Meet them before you decide to employ them.

Several companies provide private tutors and they should do the leg work of checking references and CVs as well as conducting criminal records checks. This should give you some peace of mind, but you will probably find that tutors provided by such companies are even more expensive. The other way is through private ads in local newspapers. These tend to fall into two categories; former teachers who may have now retired but enjoy the work and welcome the extra income, and students who do some teaching to help reduce their overdrafts. Former teachers should have a track record of preparing students for GCSEs. Students on the other hand are unlikely to have experience in preparing anyone for an exam, but should bring knowledge and enthusiasm to the table, and your son or daughter may be able to relate more easily to them.

Lesson 9: Use Friends And Family

If a tutor proves an expense too far, you may know someone else who could help. Perhaps you have a friend or family member who's pretty good at Maths, or can still remember some of their school Geography. Ask around to see if someone you know has a hidden talent, or a passion for a particular subject. You never know, they may be willing and able to help out. But one word of warning: the way that exam questions are set has changed dramatically over the years and someone who doesn't have recent knowledge can cause confusion.

LESSON 10: GO ONLINE

Hundreds of websites exist to give advice on specific subjects as well as general information on studying and preparing for exams. You may be surprised at how infrequently you or your son or daughter brings a text book home, but is asked to do some work from a website instead. Some courses are exclusively web-based. If you don't have internet access, most public libraries do and all schools and colleges in the UK are online. Your school, college or learning provider should provide you with a list of websites, which have been checked to ensure that they provide good quality information.

The web has revolutionised learning and can provide a great boost to any course by providing high quality materials, information and advice. This is often presented in entertaining, interactive and colourful ways, which many students enjoy. Some students still prefer books, but a lot of the material available online is very helpful, especially if you've grown up in a connected world. Have a look at You Tube. You might find worked examples of exam questions, but please be careful because the content may be unsound. You should also check the dates as there is a lot of obsolete material out there. While the web can be a great study aid, the problem is that it offers a never ending source of distractions and other things to do, from Facebook to instant messaging and Twitter. That's why it shouldn't be relied on as the sole source of study support. If you have children, give serious thought to limiting their time online.

LESSON 11: OBEY THE RULES

If your course requires you to submit some work by a certain time, or if you have to prepare for a controlled assessment task, ensure you know what is and isn't allowed. Ignorance is no excuse, so make sure that you know what's expected and don't fall foul of the rules. You may be given written instructions and it's important that you follow these and meet deadlines.

LESSON 12: PRESENT YOUR WORK WELL

Don't spoil a great piece of work by making silly mistakes. Check and double check any work that you have to hand in for assessment as part of the course. Errors can cost you marks, which may mean the difference between one grade and another or a pass and a fail. Important checks include:

- ✓ Spelling and grammar – double check that they are correct
- ✓ Details – have you left out anything important? Is your name on it, for example!
- ✓ Are the pages numbered and collected in the right order?
- ✓ Is it neat and tidy, with no stains?

If your handwriting is so bad that your teachers can't understand it, try to do something about it now. If people who know you find it difficult to understand your scrawl, what chance will an examiner have?

LESSON 13: DON'T CHEAT

Copying straight from the internet, books or other people is plagiarism, which will most likely be spotted by the teacher who marks your work. And if the teacher doesn't spot it, a moderator (from the exam board) probably will. If you indulge in a spot of plagiarism and are caught, you risk having your grade reduced or even being barred from getting a grade at all. At the end of the day, it's personal work that is being assessed – or should be – not someone else's. See chapter 7 for more on this.

COPING WITH EXAMS AND REVISION

Whatever your age and whatever subject you're taking, nerves can affect you on the big day. With controlled assessment and the introduction of modular exams – taken at different times of the year – the pressure is less when compared with the all-or-nothing few hours at the end of a two year course. Nevertheless, good preparation and planning can help to take the pressure off what can be a very stressful time.

USE A REVISION TIMETABLE

Plan in advance what you will revise and when you'll revise it with a revision timetable. Try to stick to the plan – and give yourself plenty of time by starting well before the exams do.

Practise With Past Exam Papers

Past papers are very useful and schools and colleges usually retain a stock of these. You can also purchase them or perhaps get them free from the relevant exam board. Exposure to previous exam papers early on can help to reduce nerves and the fear of the unexpected, especially if you are scared of exams. Remember to get a copy of last year's mark schemes for the subjects you're studying to see the instructions to examiners on how to award marks. Whilst past papers are very useful, they're not much help if you have no idea of the correct answers or what examiners are looking for. This is where you have to put some faith in your teachers and tutors, who are specialists in their subjects and know what different responses are worth. You should work through previous questions with your teacher or tutor and get tips on how to improve your chances of achieving a higher grade.

Take A Break

Make sure you're not in front of books or computers all of the time; relaxation is needed, as too much revision all at once will result in diminishing returns, where less and less information is retained and concentration becomes harder.

Check The Calendar

Write down all of your exam dates, times and locations. Parents may want to have their own copy.

LOOK AFTER YOURSELF

Make sure that you eat and drink properly and get enough sleep at exam time. You'll need to be alert and have enough energy. Snacking on crisps or chocolate won't help, while fatigue ruins concentration and increases frustration.

FRIENDLY SUPPORT

Some people find that revising with friends can be very effective, but pick your study partners carefully.

KEEP COOL

Some people become more argumentative than usual in the run up to exams, while others withdraw into a shell. If you're the one preparing for your exams, try to keep a sense of perspective, because if you're stressed out you can't concentrate. People develop their own style at exam time. Some stick post-it notes on walls; others fill notebooks; others talk to themselves a lot. If you're a friend or family member of someone taking exams, it can feel like being the manager of a football team who after all the training can only look on from the sidelines. You can't actually take the exam for your friend, partner, colleague or child, so you need to remain hopeful, relaxed and encouraging. It's a difficult balancing act, but some encouragement can go a long way.

COULD YOU GAIN AN ADVANTAGE?

Let's assume that you have got the date for your exam. You know how long it will last and where it will be held.

Fine, but could you qualify for extra exam time, benefit from a specially developed exam paper, or have someone read out the questions for you? The exams regulator allows these and other measures through a system called Access Arrangements. Look at Figure 7 to see how common these are.

Two things to bear in mind here:

1. You have to apply to the exam board through your learning provider, school or college – you can't apply as an individual

2. Applications need to be made in plenty of time – well before the exam is due to take place.

Schools and colleges often have specialist teachers who look after requests of this kind. The application is made online and the current regulations list 32 different access arrangements that can be made. Access arrangements are designed primarily to enable people with permanent or temporary disabilities to compete equally with their peers. If you have some kind of disability, this might be all it takes to bring your grade up. For example, a student might have to use a word processor rather than a pen.

Here is an example of a special arrangement: "Candidate's first language is not in English, Irish or Welsh, and has been in the UK less than two years prior to the date of the examination, one or more parents/carers is not British born and the candidate has not been educated in an English speaking school abroad. The use of a bi-lingual dictionary reflects the candidate's normal way of working. Allow a bi-lingual dictionary and up to a maximum of 25% extra time."

Exam board guidelines show examples of how to allocate additional time. If a candidate has moderate dyslexia, he or she may be allowed up to 25% more time – so a two hour exam would become two-and-a-half hours for this candidate. I mention dyslexia deliberately because of the recent uncomfortable growth in the numbers of students claiming the disability.

HOW COMMON ARE ACCESS ARRANGEMENTS?

Lots of people are granted extra time or another access arrangement. Let's look at some figures for 2010:

- ✓ 287,900 requests for special arrangements were made – and 94% were granted

- ✓ Nearly 110,000 requests resulted in candidates being given up to 25% extra time to finish an exam

- ✓ A further 14,856 cases allowed candidates a dictionary of some kind and extra 25% time

- ✓ 21,920 requests for modified exam papers were approved. A typical example could be to help someone with poor eyesight by printing an exam paper with large, bold text.

Figure 7 Source: Ofqual

You might be amused by one request that I had for a modified paper. One of the GCSE language papers offered was in Mandarin, a subject that is increasingly popular. However we winced when a request for a special paper was received on behalf of a candidate who had exercised his right to have his Mandarin paper written in the Welsh language! But guess what, we did it, spending considerable time and effort to ensure that the assessment was accurate and fair.

THE ROLE OF SCHOOLS AND COLLEGES

As well as the things you can do as an individual to increase your chances of achieving a better grade, there are lots of things that schools and colleges can do too. Some students do much better than others, and I really do mean *much* better. You just have to look at property prices in the area of a good school. We are used to fee-paying and selective schools being at the top, yet some state schools are also high performers. Independent providers, such as distance learning companies, often have much higher than average student results. But why, and what if anything can you do about it? As Managing Director of Edexcel I formed a personal view based on the observation of exam results and I think that there are three key factors that contribute to excellence in school performance: discipline, syllabus design and the use of technology.

DISCIPLINE

This is a fundamental for excellence. Time and again I have seen failing institutions turned around when a new head teacher or principal is backed by politicians and governors to sort out the management of the school or college. Teaching can only be successful in the right environment. Discipline is evident in all of the state schools that do well and absent from all of those that are poor. All schools have boards of governors drawn from ordinary people who care about their schools. You can make a difference by becoming a governor.

As an adult learner your choice of learning provider is also crucial, and we have seen a growth in popularity of distance learning where home study is the dominant activity. The amount and quality of support you receive throughout the course could make a big difference to how well you do. It seems a certainty that more learning in the future will be through the digital world.

The other thing you could do, if you have the time and the inclination, is to start your own school. While this would have been a laughable suggestion just a few years ago, the government's 'free schools' policy enables you to set up a state-funded yet 'independent' school. Parents, teachers, private companies and charities have all expressed an interest, so it will be interesting to see the take up over the next few years.

SYLLABUS

The syllabus covers what is taught, and it differs widely between different schools and colleges. However, the choice of what is taught and how students are streamed is often done poorly. For schools, after the compulsory GCSE subjects, they have a wealth of other qualifications to choose from. We know that about half of all students fail to gain five 'good' GCSEs, including Maths and English. Many students who struggle with traditional exams would achieve much better results by studying vocational qualifications that use continuous assessment. These are not easy options, but too many schools still look down their noses at them, believing that traditional 'academic' subjects are the only route to success. That isn't true.

TECHNOLOGY

Incredible though it may seem, schools spend huge amounts of time and money in assessing students without really understanding the detail of performance. In 2005 the exam board Edexcel launched a massive programme of analysis called Results Plus. It enabled students' and teachers' performances to be analysed in detail. It showed what was understood and what wasn't, and what was being taught well by the teacher – and where more work was needed. It helped streaming and was available for every subject. The other major exam boards are slowly developing similar technology. Sadly, few schools exploit this system, but those that do have seen dramatic improvements in performance. Ask your school about Results Plus or the alternatives. Ask about the comparative performance of the teachers. Ask to see the analysis for your son or daughter (it is freely available online to all schools). The response you get will tell you something.

Chapter 7

CHEAT!
HOW CHEATING IS DONE, HOW IT'S SPOTTED – AND THE CONSEQUENCES OF GETTING CAUGHT

'Cheats never prosper' is a phrase that most of our parents, grandparents and teachers have probably used at some time; you may have said it yourself. But is it true in the world of exams? Concerns about cheating – or the potential for cheating – led the exam regulators to put coursework in the bin of educational history and encouraged many fee paying schools to move to International GCSEs, where coursework is non-existent. The chance for mums, dads, brothers, sisters and even teachers, to lend a helping hand led many to question the accuracy and merit of the grade awarded.

Coursework undoubtedly offered the chance for coaching and copying, with allegations of plagiarism widespread. Research published by the Cranfield School of Management in 2009 found that more than 28% of students believed it was "acceptable" to copy information from the internet and almost one in six admitted to cheating in their homework by using the internet. When you look at the figures, achievement in coursework tended to be higher than exams, although that doesn't prove that cheating actually took place.

The official figures show cheating in coursework to be rare, although it is difficult to prove. Coursework was always marked by teachers, who were responsible for policing the system, as they must now supervise coursework's replacement, controlled assessment. Under the new rules, students will still be able to do research outside of the classroom; it's just that the finished product must be completed under some sort of supervision.

The regulator, Ofqual, collects statistics for the numbers and types of cheating that occur and these statistics confirm the very low instances of cheating, including plagiarism. Ofqual describes cheating as malpractice and the description includes offences by schools' management and individual teachers as well as students. The numbers only cover the incidents that resulted in the application of a penalty where evidence of malpractice was confirmed. In the summer of 2010, 4,131 penalties were issued, but this number compares with over 15 million exam papers set and marked! Year on year the numbers of penalties has been steadily reducing. If you think about cheating as a battle between the cheats, perhaps armed with new technology, and the exam boards with rigorous process and detection capability, then you might conclude that the good guys are winning.

The most common cause of penalties, nearly half of the total number, is where candidates bring 'unauthorised' material into the exam room. Mobile phones and other electronic devices account for 1,377 penalties alone in this category, and easily top the league table of cheating. Next comes plagiarism with 860 penalties or 21% of the total number. Disruptive behaviour and passing information make the top five of the cheating league tables, but surprisingly, a place in the top five goes to obscenity; 9% of all penalties arise from inappropriate, offensive or obscene material. 'Street language' sometimes used in exam papers by students who are reflecting their normal communication style is an issue that causes debate.

It's not just students who cheat however; in summer 2010 exam boards issued 106 penalties to schools and colleges, mainly because of lax security or inappropriate assistance to candidates. Separately, 79 penalties were issued to individual staff and these were dominated by instances of inappropriate student assistance. However the incidents were serious enough for 13 staff members to be suspended from all future involvement in exams or assessments.

In the summer of 2010 Ofqual changed the way it reported malpractice, producing a less detailed schedule of offences and penalties. Figure 8 shows the detailed statistics of candidate malpractice for the summer exams in 2009 and it is very similar in shape to that of summer 2010, although overall numbers have reduced. Figure 8 is interesting because it shows the penalties issued in each case.

Candidate malpractice totals for the three major UK exam boards in 2009	Numbers of students			
Type of offence	Warning	Loss of marks	Loss of certificate	Total
The alteration of any results document, including certificates	1	0	1	2
A breach of instructions or advice of an invigilator, supervisor, or the exam board in relation to the examination rules and regulations	20	7	2	29
Failing to abide by the conditions of supervision designated to maintain the security of the examinations	16	11	29	56
Collusion: working collaboratively with other candidates beyond what is permitted	36	30	11	77
Copying from another candidate (including the misuse of ICT)	60	88	39	187
The deliberate destruction of work	1	1	6	8
Disruptive behaviour in the examination room or assessment session (including the use of offensive language)	93	297	87	477
Talking	44	83	8	135
Written communication	10	5	2	17
Making a false declaration of authenticity	1	1	4	6

Misuse of, or attempted misuse of, examination material and resources	0	0	1	1
Bringing into the exam room notes in the wrong format or prohibited annotations	3	1	1	5
The inclusion of inappropriate, offensive or obscene material in scripts, coursework or portfolios	135	65	25	225
Impersonation	0	0	2	2
Plagiarism: unacknowledged copying from published sources (including the internet); incomplete referencing	32	137	17	186
Theft (where the candidate's work is removed or stolen)	0	1	4	5
Introducing unauthorised notes, study guides and personal organisers	29	58	35	122
Introducing own blank paper	1	0	0	1
Using calculators, dictionaries (when prohibited)	3	16	0	19
Personal stereo (including MP3, iPod) or and other similar electronic devices	34	13	1	48
Mobile phone or other electronic communicating devices	364	564	101	1029
Behaving in a way as to undermine the integrity of the examination.	0	0	1	1
Total number of candidates penalised	2638		

Figure 8 Source: Ofqual

The table confirms that mobile phones and their derivatives are the real danger, accounting for 39% of all candidate malpractice, with 101 students losing grades and 564 having marks deducted. Disruptive behaviour was penalised heavily. The inclusion of inappropriate, offensive or obscene material (often in coursework) was high and it is surprising how often street obscenities are included in candidate submissions. Although 2,638 candidates were caught cheating, this represents a tiny proportion of the total number taking exams and we should be proud of the integrity of the assessment arrangements in schools and colleges. Plagiarism certainly featured but it was by no means the most significant offence in terms of penalties and only 17 candidates lost grades as a result.

Sometimes cheating can be as simple as not referencing work properly, leading to students losing marks. This is an important lesson if you're doing research for a piece of work that will be assessed. Passing off ideas and arguments as your own and not referencing the material properly could land you in hot water. Bear in mind that if an examiner finds anomalies or inconsistencies in a teacher's marks, it is possible that the whole year group's marks could be pulled down. While this may seem unfair, it reflects the lack of confidence in that school's or college's ability to prevent cheating. Parents should take an active interest in how the school is run as it could be your child that suffers, even if they've done nothing wrong. Plagiarism can be detected by special software used by exam boards, although this can be harder to detect in handwritten pieces of work. If the material is accessible to the student, it's accessible to the teachers and examiners as well, so there's a decent chance of discovery.

A HELPING HAND?

So what is an 'acceptable' amount of help for friends and family to give students when they are researching and preparing work that will count towards their final exam grades? I think it's fair enough to offer help and make suggestions, so long as the actual work is completed by the student. We shouldn't be expected to enter a silent order and not discuss our work with anyone. You'd expect, and should perhaps encourage, students to collaborate in their studies with their friends and share what they've discovered. In the early years of secondary school, in particular, students are often encouraged to work in pairs or groups, so it's not uncommon. Online research isn't always as easy as we might think; we sometimes have to wade through a huge amount of dross before reaching quality material. So taking a keen interest, supporting, questioning and making suggestions is fine; just make sure that the person producing the work is the one who gets it down on paper and understands what has been written down.

The same question applies to teachers and tutors, whose job it is to coach and help, but who must also monitor, supervise and mark the work. The vast majority are able to draw the line between helping a student to develop a good piece of work and actually directing how the work is done. Discovering cheating by a teacher is very rare, although as

I've mentioned, inconsistencies in marking the work can lead to problems.

How People Cheat

Exams officers have to get to grips with highly complex documents, rules and regulations to ensure that exams are run fairly and efficiently in their schools and colleges. Rules exist for every aspect of the examination process, from storing exam papers securely when they arrive in school before the big day, to the minimum distance allowed between desks in the exam hall, to the infamous 'you can turn your paper over and begin' at the start of each exam. All of these rules are designed to prevent cheating and ensure a level playing field, with no-one gaining an unfair advantage.

As a student or parent you should be reassured that a huge amount of time, effort and money is put into ensuring that cheats won't prosper and that all of your studying and revision won't be blown away by someone who knew the questions in advance. But as in most spheres of life, money can be made by the unscrupulous, and that may include examiners and teachers as well as friends and relatives. We put a great deal of trust in the thousands of people who mark exams every year as they usually see the questions in advance. Overwhelmingly that trust is repaid and there is scant evidence of cheating by examiners. The risk is reduced still further by the fact that many examiners only see a limited number of questions – the ones they are personally asked to mark – rather than the whole question paper. Technology has enabled this change and you can read more about the way exams are marked in chapter 9.

OLD SCHOOL, NEW SCHOOL – SAME OLD STORY

Cheating in exams takes many forms – and they have multiplied with the growth of electronic mobile devices – but whatever name you give it, the penalties for cheating can be severe. Types of cheating in exams include:

- ✓ Writing on sleeves, clothing and skin

- ✓ Using a calculator when one isn't allowed

- ✓ Mobile devices used to store or download information, including mobile phones, iPods and other mp3 players

- ✓ Mobile devices used to relay information via an earpiece

- ✓ Revision notes hidden in a toilet, which is visited during the exam

- ✓ Impostors taking the exam for someone else

- ✓ Stolen exam papers giving advance notice of the questions

- ✓ Disruption and diversion

However, examiners do have unique, privileged access to the content of secret exam papers and many conduct advice sessions laid on by the exam boards. The regulator views this activity with increasing concern and at the end of 2011 required an exam paper to be withdrawn and replaced after secret filming by a newspaper revealed that a senior examiner had gone too far when 'coaching' teachers.

MOBILE MISTAKE

One message that you should get into your head is that no mobile device of any kind is allowed into the exam hall. Anyone found with a mobile phone or an iPod risks being excluded and having their whole exam paper voided, so taking one in could be a fatal error. However, as mobile devices become smaller, more powerful and more sophisticated, some people will probably continue to take the risk.

IS THAT REALLY YOU?

While impostors are not a problem in state schools, they have been known to sit exams. This may happen if a student has gone to a specialist or 'crammer' school, but decided that they still don't know enough to be sure of passing. They may then pay someone to turn up in their place to sit the exam whilst pretending to be them. In these cases, students usually take exams at recognised centres, such as schools and colleges, where the staff don't know the person concerned. Adults studying courses by distance learning also have to attend schools or colleges in this way to sit their exams. In such cases, those invigilating the exams only have a name; they have no idea what the candidate looks like and photographic identity is rarely used.

DELIBERATE DISRUPTION

One little known way in which some students try to gain an advantage is by deliberately disrupting the exam. Sometimes this may be by saying that they are too hot or too cold; that there's too much noise outside, that they don't feel well or that they need to use the toilet. Schools and colleges have rules for dealing with this kind of thing, but it can lead to whoever is supervising the exam allowing everyone some extra time – say an additional 5-10 minutes – at their discretion. This could be exactly what the person wanted.

THE INTERNATIONAL DIMENSION

Exam boards have international examination businesses and during the exam season have candidates taking the same exam all over the world. This means that if an exam is due to start at 9.30am, it must start at the same time wherever you are in the world – so that could be 5.30pm in Hong Kong or 4.30am in Peru! By and large, exam centres stick to the rules, but if they don't and an exam is taken before it's supposed to, then the paper is 'public' and there's a risk that the questions could appear in online forums. This is a risk that is kept under constant review by exam boards. Some students do take their examinations early but they must be kept in isolation after they have finished their exam until one hour after the exam start time in the UK.

SEEING THE QUESTIONS IN ADVANCE

This usually happens for one of two reasons.

Firstly, theft. Unfortunately it's not uncommon for mail vans to be robbed or stolen, and while the thieves may not have been particularly happy at finding sack loads of exam question papers you might expect them to exploit the opportunity.

Secondly, cock-up. Exam boards and the examiners they employ (mostly teachers and ex-teachers) make mistakes. So sometimes an exam paper, or some exam questions, may be inadvertently attached to an email, which is then forwarded, copied, etc...and the rest is history.

Thankfully, both events are rare, but they do happen. In these circumstances, the regulator usually demands that the particular exam paper is scrapped and replaced by another one. This is a right royal pain, but it's a contingency that all exam boards must plan for. The cost goes up, examiners need to be trained to mark a new exam paper, and it's a logistical nightmare, but it has to be done.

However, if someone has obtained an exam paper in advance, they're often tracked down with a forensic precision that would make Sherlock Holmes beam with pride. In Edexcel, for example, a former policeman headed up the Compliance Unit for many years and was responsible for looking into cheating allegations. Perhaps unsurprisingly, those found with stolen papers are not master criminals and a search of their bags often finds a raft of other stolen material; the police are involved and it's bad news all round. Curiously, possessing an exam paper in advance of the exam is not a criminal matter unless it's been obtained through a robbery or break-in. It is an offence to copy and distribute exam papers, although this is a matter for the civil, not the criminal law.

While the chances of this happening are rare, you should note that if you or someone you know is offered an exam paper in advance, there's a 90% chance that it's a fake. Exam boards investigate many allegations every year and most don't stand up to scrutiny. Enterprising individuals mock up question papers, which are then sold by school bullies or fraudsters. I've heard of unsuspecting students being forced to hand over £80 for fake exam papers, while the going rate for the genuine article a few days in advance of exam day could be as much as £500. Circulation of these papers is often limited to small geographical areas, with exam papers sometimes sold at football matches the weekend before the exam. By this time, the value has gone down, and if an exam paper appears on the internet, then its sell-on value drops to zero. If you or someone you know is offered an exam paper 'in advance' the best advice is to report it to the school, the regulator or the exam board. Such allegations can present teachers with a problem as they reflect badly on the school. My own experience is that schools may not be quick to report a rumour until they're sure that it has some substance.

THE STING

At Edexcel, we investigated several allegations that an exam paper had been made available in advance within a school or local community – possibly due to an unscrupulous teacher opening the paper in advance and sharing the contents.

To deal with this, we've mounted sting operations. One of these worked like this:

- ✓ We contacted all the schools in the suspect region to let them know we'd discovered an error in an imminent exam paper and would deliver a replacement just ahead of the exam

- ✓ The new paper was delivered by a member of Edexcel's staff on exam day giving time for the school or college to administer the exam properly

- ✓ This 'new' paper was actually exactly the same as the old one, but with one of the questions subtly altered – let's call it question 7 – it looked very like the old version but the correct answer would be different from the original.

After the exam was taken the completed papers were delivered to specially nominated examiners who routinely marked the papers, but who were unaware of the sting.

When the modified exam papers were marked and we found that a number of students had produced the right answer to the *original* question 7 – but the wrong answer to the new one – we had the evidence we needed to prove that they could only have given that response if they had seen the original paper in advance.

THANK YOU MISS MONEYPENNY – HIGH SECURITY FOR HIGH STAKES EXAMS

By their very nature, exams in the UK are secret; you don't know what you're going to be asked until you're in the exam room. The integrity of individual exams and the exam system in general is crucial. For this reason, the lengths to which exam boards go to protect the integrity of this system borders on something out of a spy novel. For example, regulators have seriously considered electronically screening exam rooms to prevent data being transmitted via mobile devices. Part of the problem faced by schools and colleges is that invigilators – the people supervising exams – may not be teachers, but are brought in especially for the occasion. Without wishing to indulge in ageist stereotypes, it's probably true that older people who often carry out this role may not always be fully aware of the full potential that digital technology offers to the determined cheat.

Today, some high stakes exams, such as the Driving Theory Test, use a wide range of security devices to prevent cheating, ranging from iris recognition, fingerprinting and CCTV in the test centre. Regrettably, I have little doubt that some of this technology will encroach upon school and college-based exams in years to come. Other ways of reducing the risk of cheating include the delivery of exam papers to schools and colleges in sealed, tamper-proof bags. All of the exam boards pay for an inspection team to do spot checks to ensure that schools and colleges are following the regulations for safe and secure storage. Exam boards have experimented with various ways of finding malpractice over the years and continue to do so. One of these has included the use of radio frequency ID tags like those placed on CDs and other items to ensure you don't walk out of the store without paying. Software designed to detect plagiarism, pre-prepared answers and other forms of cheating is also high on the priority list, helped by the fact that so many exams are now marked on screen.

TESTING ON SCREEN

As technology improves, some exams will be taken on screen rather than on paper. Whilst using a computer to take an exam won't cause a problem for most people, it creates additional headaches for exam boards and regulators. Some parts of exams are already taken on computer. While this is still small scale, and often used for multiple choice questions, it is a way of testing that is likely to expand, bringing new challenges to try to prevent cheating. Could students see the screen next to them? Could the school's computer system be hacked, enabling the unscrupulous to see the questions in advance? Exam boards would have to prove that the on-screen exam was set at exactly the same level as the paper version, as there would always have to be paper versions as back-up in case school IT systems failed. That is difficult because some students perform much better on computer than on paper.

To move to on-screen testing we would have to shift away from the idea of a secret exam taken by everyone at the same time, and move to a system based on a question bank. In this system a very large number of questions are set and some are delivered randomly to the student being tested. This type of system is used by some professional bodies and often these questions are available in advance, as with the driving theory test. The regulator has no plans to implement computer-based assessment for so-called 'high stakes' exams, such as GCSEs and A-levels. I think that the traditional secret exam paper taken with pen and paper will be with us for several years to come. Education moves slowly.

THE CONSEQUENCES OF GETTING CAUGHT

When someone is found to have cheated, or is suspected of cheating, the major exam boards use an independent panel to review allegations. This is made up of ex-teachers and others who know how the system works, but none of them is directly employed by an exam board.

The bottom line is that they try to make the punishment fit the crime. For example, a student may have marks deducted from a particular exam paper if they brought a mobile phone into the exam room, but there's no evidence that they used it, or intended to use it, to gain an advantage. But if they've cheated using an mp3 player or a crib sheet it's possible that the entire paper will be void and they won't even be awarded a grade. This is almost certainly the punishment if a copy of the exam paper has been found in advance. In the most serious cases, it's possible for individuals to be banned from taking any UK-based exam for a number of years. This is usually reserved for those individuals who have been dealing in stolen exam papers. One such group did just that in North London a few years ago, with a corrupt deputy head at the centre of a ring that was copying and distributing a large number of exam papers for money. Schools can also be punished if the management is found to be complicit in corrupt practices and some small 'crammer'-type establishments have been prevented from offering exams from any UK exam board – although this has never happened to a state school.

Just Say No

In the face of temptation, it's easy to give in, but the best advice is 'don't'. I know of several cases where students would probably have achieved a grade A under their own steam, but whose exam result was voided because of an infringement. Cheating tarnishes your individual record and may come back to haunt you later in life. At A-level, it has cost many capable students a place at university.

Chapter 8

'EXAMS ARE GETTING EASIER.' DISCUSS

I f you are taking exams, or are the parent or partner of someone who is, then media reporting of results day can't be much fun. Every summer it seems that standards are falling and the results aren't worth the paper they're printed on. The pundits gleefully point to ever-rising pass rates as evidence that exams are being 'dumbed down'. Here is a typical example.

"Her Majesty's Inspectors of Schools have suggested for the first time that standards at GCSE are falling. Their report shocked teachers and delighted right-wingers yesterday..."

Sounds familiar? Well this quote comes from the Independent on Sunday dated 2 September 1992, just four years after the very first GCSE results in 1988! Criticism of A-levels, GCSEs, and educational standards in general goes back a very long way. In this chapter I want to explain why the popular idea of falling standards is ever present and offer a few views on the reality behind the rhetoric. But let's start with the perception problem.

How Exams Used To Be Graded – Every Year The same

In chapters 2 and 3 I described how GCSEs and A-levels were graded before the current system was introduced in the year 2000. The old system was known as 'Norm Referencing' and ranked students according to performance. While this was simple and easy to understand, it was impossible to tell whether teaching and learning were getting better – or worse. Every year the same percentage of students was awarded an A, and the same percentage awarded an E. Tough luck if the candidates in your year were brighter than in the previous year, because the percentage of top grades was fixed and you would have to do better in a 'bright' year to get that top grade. However, this system not only looked fair, it felt fair. It put students in competition with each other and separated them according to their exam performance. An A grade was relatively rare and thus had intrinsic value. It placed an A grade student well ahead of the crowd – literally, in the top 10% or thereabouts for each subject.

How Exams Are Graded Today – Jump That Hurdle

The new method of awarding grades is known as criterion referencing. Put simply, this involves setting fixed levels or hurdles for grades, so student performance can be measured year-on-year. If a student receives enough marks for the grade, then that grade is awarded, irrespective of how many students achieve it. In this way, so the thinking goes, government can measure whether standards are improving and schools and colleges can be held to account.

One way to think about the difference between the old and current ways of awarding grades is to compare exams with the Olympic high jump event. To be selected for your country you have to be able to jump a minimum height, usually during a series of special trials. In the year 2000 Olympic Games the men's qualifying height was 2.3 metres, and everyone who cleared that height was allowed to compete – they had 'qualified'. This notion is similar to the way that GCSE and A-level grades are awarded now. If the qualifying standard is achieved then the award is made. However, some years before the year 2000, the qualifying height was much lower. Dick Fosbury (of 'Fosbury Flop' fame, where the athlete cleared the bar backwards for the first time) actually won the event in the 1968 Olympics with a jump of 2.24 metres. On that performance he wouldn't have qualified for the Games in 2000 because he wouldn't have been good enough to compete!

Here then is the problem of setting a fixed standard. Whilst the Olympic committee reviews its qualifying standard for every new Games – quite literally setting the bar higher for the high jump – the UK educational establishment has attempted to keep the GCSE and A-level standard – the 'height of the bar' – at the same level for years. This means that it is possible for a large number of students to gain the top grades, so long as they can meet the fixed level. And guess what has happened? More and more students do achieve the top grades every year. Over time, teaching methods, exam techniques and support materials have improved, helping more and more students to gain the higher awards. But for those of us brought up on the old system of a fixed percentage for each grade, large and increasing numbers of students gaining the highest grades feels wrong.

Yet we know that in every walk of life, people continue to outperform their predecessors. In 1953 Mount Everest was climbed for the first time. Now ascents of the mountain are commonplace. Did the summit become smaller? Has Mount Everest been dumbed down? Or did climbing equipment, techniques, training and a host of other improvements enable more people to achieve the ascent? If we agree that these improvements are crucial, then we could argue that improved teaching and learning have helped more people to reach the educational summit of top grades. I'm sure that this is the case, but there's more to it than that.

LIES, DAMNED LIES AND STATISTICS

The headlines suggest that things have changed dramatically, although perceptions can often be confused by statistics. If we look at comparisons over time for students taking several subjects, it is true that the top grades have increased. Figure 9 shows the findings of a study by the Joint Council for Qualifications. This compared the grades achieved by two groups of 30 students from the same backgrounds, each of whom took eight GCSEs. So the total number of grades awarded to each group was 240 (30 students times 8 GCSEs).

It shows that the number of students achieving A* to C increased, while the numbers awarded grade D and below fell. In this context, it's worth remembering the government's relentless drive to increase the number of students gaining five or more GCSE passes at grades A* to C as a measure of each school's success.

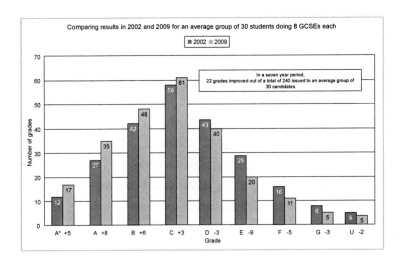

Figure 9

While only 22 grades improved out of a possible 240 (just over 9%) over a seven year period, you can see that the change was all at the top end, with 41.6% more A* grades awarded and almost 30% more A grades. Although this was a small sample of students, it does mirror the national trend.

The obvious conclusion is that, far from dumbing down, the improvement in pass rates should be much better than it actually is. An improvement in only 22 grades is arguably poor – even more students should be getting A grades!

OTHER FACTORS THAT AFFECT GRADES

The different system for awarding grades is crucial in accounting for the steady growth in students achieving higher grades. But when you examine the reasons for the growing number of A grades, you'll see that it isn't the only factor. Let's look at some of the others.

COURSEWORK

If a subject includes coursework, the evidence suggests that students do better than on subjects that are simply measured by exams. As we have seen, coursework has inspired many professional debates about its value to learning, but there is a correlation here. As coursework is introduced or withdrawn, overall grade performance tends to change. So the withdrawal of coursework from GCSEs from 2009 onwards and its replacement with controlled assessment will have an impact on exam results. We just don't yet know how big that impact will be.

CHOICE

Another major contributor to the growing number of top grades is choice. During recent years the number of GCSE and A-level subjects has grown. Students can choose the subjects that they are more likely to do well in and avoid the subjects they don't like, or are taught by unpopular teachers. For example, in 2004 the requirement for school children to take a foreign language at GCSE was scrapped. As a result, we've seen a big fall in the number of entries for languages, but performance has improved as they tend to be chosen by people with motivation and ability.

GCSE EQUIVALENCE

Another factor that tends to confuse people in the exam standards debate is the way that school league table calculations differ from actual GCSE performance. Some qualifications that are not GCSEs are assigned 'GCSE equivalent' values because they are deemed to be about the same level of difficulty. These include vocational qualifications, such as BTECs. As these qualifications grow in popularity and the proportion of pupils taking them increases, they can influence the league tables.

The exam board, Edexcel, published a study estimating that BTEC equivalents alone contributed a rise of 6.68% to the numbers gaining five good GCSEs in league tables. However, the government has said that it intends to address the anomalies that result in 'GCSE equivalent' qualifications taking their place in school league tables, so watch this space.

MODULAR EXAMS

Modular exams have been part of A-levels for years and were introduced for GCSEs in 2010. We traditionally think of exams as single written papers taken at the end of the teaching year, but modular exams are different. Think of a module as a 'chunk' of learning, like algebra in Maths or Shakespeare in English Literature. Instead of these being part of the final, end of year exam, students take an exam in each separate module and their overall grade is awarded by adding together the separate module results.

For GCSE, this will probably lead to even more A grades. How can I be so sure? This is what's happened with A-levels.

Modular exams redistribute workload and revision time as each module is examined soon after studying it. This means that what is studied should be fresher in the mind, helping to memorise key facts. It is possible to re-sit modules later (although only one re-sit is generally allowed), and to focus on areas of strength. Taken together, the move to modular exams should make it easier to achieve higher grades. Can you hear the fury of the critics?

But while debates about modular exams will probably rage on for some time, we shouldn't condemn them out of hand. Let's think about what they are trying to achieve. You may have already taken a well known modular assessment – the UK driving test. This consists of a formal 'theory' exam and a practical demonstration. The UK driving test is a fixed standard, so if you achieve it, you will be granted a full driving licence. Candidates can attempt the test as many times as they like. If re-sits were not allowed, then about half of those behind the wheel right now would not be driving – including the 2009 Formula 1 World Champion, Jenson Button! If you passed the test on your third attempt, are you a worse driver than one who passed first time? Is the standard of driving degraded by allowing re-sits? You'll have your own views, but the argument that exams are so much easier today isn't as straightforward as some of the critics would have you think.

Whatever your views, the present government's policy is inclined towards traditional pen-and-paper exams taken at the end of the course. Modular exams are on the way out, certainly for GCSEs, for courses starting in September 2012. This will mean that students won't be able to re-sit individual modules at different times of the year. Also around this time, additional marks will be available for spelling, punctuation and grammar in four GCSE subjects: English Literature, Geography, History and Religious Studies. All of these changes are bound to have an impact on grades.

IS COMPETITION DRIVING DOWN STANDARDS?

Critics claim that competition amongst exam boards is boosting grades with no improvement in quality. The argument goes that as exam boards seek a bigger share of the market, they'll do almost anything to ensure students achieve better marks – thereby ensuring that schools, colleges and other learning providers choose them.

As outlined earlier, the exam system in England, Wales and Northern Ireland is unique. Schools and colleges in the state sector are funded by their local councils to deliver a national curriculum. They use some of this money to buy courses of study in different subjects, including teaching materials, examinations and supporting administration. They buy these from competing exam boards, with the decision-maker typically the head of subject in each school. But the one criterion that can't be used during the decision to buy is that of the difficulty – or easiness – of the exam. Exam boards are not allowed by the regulators to reduce standards to win business. After each set of exams, the regulators check the pass rates in each subject by each exam board to ensure that parity is maintained and that the standard is not raised or lowered.

In my experience, exam boards do not compete on 'difficulty' or 'easiness' when setting exam papers; that was certainly a strong culture during my term of office. You will not find a teacher or head teacher admitting that exam boards were chosen on the basis of 'easiness'. However, media coverage in December 2011 that exposed a small number of senior examiners seeming to call this into question has undermined confidence in the setting of exam papers and that confidence will have to be restored. The regulator is due to report on the health of the qualifications market in mid-2013 and its findings could lead to changes.

Exam boards certainly do compete strongly on help and support to teachers. This should have the effect of driving up the quality of materials and guidance. Think about it this way: exam boards should demonstrate that they set exams at a constant standard, designed to establish student ability in different subjects. If they are failing to do this then the regulator is either incompetent or weak. If they are succeeding, why shouldn't exam boards help students – and their teachers – to try to gain good grades? After all, is that not a key reason for investing in education?

If there were no league tables there would be no arguments. Nevertheless many in education argue that this situation has encouraged 'teaching to the test' and that too much effort is put into exam preparation.

ARE EXAM QUESTIONS GETTING EASIER?

One issue that excites the experts is the notion that exam questions are easier these days. It's certainly true that the way questions were set during the 1980s, for example, is different from those for current exams. Many factors contributed to this gradual change – look at the answers to the following 'exam questions' to find out more.

QUESTION: WHO RAN EXAM BOARDS UNTIL THE 1980S AND WHAT IMPACT DID THIS HAVE?

Answer: Until the 1980s, exam boards were run by universities. This meant in practice that the qualifications were targeted at the top 40% of O-level students (the precursor to GCSE) – and less than that for A-levels. This focus on brighter students meant that exam questions tended to be more open ended, requiring essay-type answers.

QUESTION: HOW HAVE EXAM QUESTIONS EVOLVED?

Answer: You may be surprised to hear that multiple choice questions were introduced in the 1970s, and were even used for subjects like English. Like GCSEs, O-levels had questions that were sub-divided into sections to help students build an answer, although there was still a requirement for extended writing.

QUESTION: WHAT IMPACT DID THE INTRODUCTION OF GCSEs HAVE ON THE TYPE OF EXAM QUESTIONS SET BY EXAMINERS?

Answer: With the scrapping of O-levels and CSEs, exam boards introduced tiers into the new GCSE to account for the different ability levels of students. Some GCSEs initially had three tiers instead of the two that most have today – while others had just one. This led to question types ranging from very structured, short answer questions for the less able students, to blank paper answer booklets for essay-type answers for the brighter students. By the 1990s all exam boards used two tiers for most subjects.

QUESTION: WHAT IMPACT DID THE INTRODUCTION OF TWO TIERS FOR MOST GCSE SUBJECTS HAVE ON SCHOOLS?

Answer: Schools were able to decide late into the academic year what tier to enter the middle ability students for. This meant that the style of the exam at each tier could not be too different. As a result, exam boards have moved most of their exams to structured questions in question-and-answer booklets.

QUESTION: RECENT GOVERNMENTS HAVE FOCUSED ON PUSHING UP THE NUMBER OF PUPILS WITH AT LEAST 'FIVE GOOD GCSEs AT GRADES A* TO C'. WHAT IMPACT HAS THIS HAD ON THE EXAM SYSTEM?

Answer: This led to a demand for exam questions that were 'C-grade friendly' – including higher tier papers that would identify the top grades but which, crucially, were accessible for the C grade student. Questions were designed that tested the more difficult content, but which were structured in a way – using sub-sections, for example – that would allow the C grade student to gain some of the marks. This in turn has had an impact on the type of questions asked of A-level students.

ARE SOME SUBJECTS EASIER THAN OTHERS?

We've already seen that some of the UK's top universities clearly believe that there are 'soft' subjects at A-level. Their representative, the Russell Group, issued guidance on the issue in 2011. As ever, you should check the admission rules for your subject and university very carefully before making choices. But you, and, perhaps, some of our institutions, should be careful about jumping to conclusions too quickly.

Bear in mind how the media report A-level results. Look at the results for Maths in summer 2011 for instance: 97.6% of students gained an A-level, and you could be forgiven for thinking that every exam leads to overwhelming success.

The trouble is that we don't have the notion of 'pass' and 'fail' any more. You should ask yourself what value an A-level at grade E is really worth, because while this is still a 'pass', the reality is that it won't impress too many universities or employers.

In Figure 10, taken from the A-level summer exams in 2011, I have selected three so-called 'hard' and 'soft' subjects side by side. If you were trying to choose an easy subject on the basis of historical performance, the easiest subjects appear to be Maths, Physics and English, as these are the ones with the most A grades! Media Studies seems to be the most difficult to get top marks in, with just 13.4% of students awarded an A* or A, yet this is always a subject that gets a bashing as one of the 'soft' subjects that more and more students choose to boost their grades.

Subject	Cumulative percentages awarded by grade							
	Total entry	A*	A	B	C	D	E	U
Maths	82,995	17.8	44.7	66.4	81.8	92.0	97.6	100
Media, Film, TV Studies	33,855	1.6	11.8	42.8	78.7	95.3	99.1	100
Physics	32,860	10.4	33.0	55.2	73.5	88.0	96.7	100
Performing Arts	3,575	4.7	16.8	46.9	77.6	94.4	99.3	100
English	89,980	7.1	22.3	49.4	78.6	95.2	99.4	100
Sport / PE subjects	19,344	4.4	15.2	36.5	62.1	84.2	96.9	100

Figure 10 Source: Joint Council for Qualifications

THE APPLIANCE OF SCIENCE

GCSE Science is one area where the standards debate really took hold.

In 2009, Lord May of Oxford, the then president-elect of the British Science Association, said efforts to make science subjects more attractive and accessible for pupils had resulted in a curriculum with too much "waffle" and exams which have replaced key mathematical skills and problem solving with less demanding questions.

Baroness Warnock said that science GCSEs were more "fit for the pub" than the classroom, while Dr Richard Pyke, the Chief Executive of the Royal Society of Chemistry, said the GCSE would disadvantage state school pupils because their private school counterparts were still studying separate Physics, Chemistry and Biology. Dr Pike said: "The science community has identified entire science papers with no underlying Maths, and science questions with no science. This is a blatant breach of expected standards." He called for exam boards to be fined, adding: "A million pound surcharge would focus the mind of any examining board chief executive and overnight would do more than years of 'discussion between stakeholders'." How true.

One more: Sir Martin Taylor, vice-president of the Royal Society: "If we have science exams that do not test the quality of mathematics needed to do good science or if we have questions that do not require scientific knowledge to answer them then we do not have an examination system that is fit for purpose."

All damning stuff, which eventually led the regulator, Ofqual, to describe Science GCSE as "clearly a cause for concern" and demanding that students from now on would have to "... demonstrate a greater degree of mathematical knowledge, understanding and skills than is typically used in current GCSE sciences examinations".

But what was behind all of this? Well it is correct that something had changed in science. Government and the scientific community had been concerned at the falling numbers of science students at GCSE and concluded that science was dull. Through their agent, the Qualifications and Curriculum Authority, government set out to make science 'cool', leading to new criteria being issued to the competing exam boards to create curriculum materials and assessments that would attract more students.

This is a long way from the erroneous view expressed by Dr Hilary Leevers of the lobby group, the Campaign for Science and Engineering (Case), who said:

"Awarding bodies compete for custom among schools, and the schools, in turn, compete in the league tables, so there has been a driving down of standards." As a scientist, you might have expected the good doctor to have a firmer grasp of cause and effect.

Alas, cool science did not find favour with the institutions, despite the fact that it did attract more students. To add to the problem, the heavy demands of health and safety legislation have meant the removal of some of the more exciting, practical engagement with the real world.

So now it's back to the future as science will once again become, no doubt, rather more dull – but worthy, let's hope, of the esteem of our esteemed institutions.

PERCEPTION AND REALITY – WHEN IS A 'STANDARD' NOT A 'STANDARD'?

Civil servants, politicians, regulators and, of course exam boards, all claim that standards have not been reduced, and that the improvement in grades is the result of hard work by the teachers and students, and increased investment in education. (It is interesting to note that no-one seems to claim very loudly that students might be getting brighter). I have publicly maintained the view that standards have been held. So who is right? After all, if you are an investor in education through your taxes, you have a right to know. As the head of an exam board, my signature can be found at the bottom of quite literally millions of exam certificates, maybe even one of yours. I was one of just three people in England authorised to sign A-level and GCSE certificates. I followed the regulator's Code of Practice with diligence and did everything I could to maintain grade standards over time. Detailed records prove it.

SO HAVE STANDARDS FALLEN?

Yes, I think they probably have. But before you reach for the telephone to call your MP, read the next few paragraphs.

What's crucial here is the perception and experience of many people outside of education. In 2011 just over 30% of students taking GCSE History were awarded a grade A* or A. No amount of explanation by academics and experts can change the perception that something is wrong with so many students being awarded the top grades. No amount of technical data can convince us that standards have been maintained if the experience of employers is that many school leavers are not equipped with basic skills. In an exam graded A* to E or G we intuitively expect to see only a few at the top.

So how can I claim that I maintained standards, yet believe that standards have fallen? Actually, it's not so difficult, because the education establishment that I was part of uses the term 'standard' in a very specific way. Let me explain. The most common use of the word 'standard' is to describe levels of excellence in different fields. We talk about a hotel having high standards, and know what that means: it is significantly better than the others. So educational standards are generally thought of in similar terms, where teachers teach well, students work hard, exam results are good and the school or college is a credit to the community. We could use the term 'excellence' instead of 'standard' here. Those of us outside of education tend to think of the word 'standard' in relative rather than absolute terms. A high standard is thought of as one that differentiates the best. Intuitively everything can't be at a high standard.

However, in the world of education, the term 'standard' is often used specifically to refer to a defined level – a fixed performance. In the earlier example of the high jump, the qualifying 'standard' was set at 2.3 metres; jump it, and you've met the standard. This is how educationalists use the term – and the government has held the fixed standard for A-levels and GCSEs for more than ten years. As a result many more students attain higher grades than before. One more twist. Far from bemoaning the numbers of students getting good grades, perhaps we should have expected even better performance than we have achieved. The increase in the numbers of high grades should have been greater – the improvement is at best modest. If you look again at Figure 9 at the beginning of this chapter, the analysis showed the results of 240 grades awarded. Seven years later, only 22 of 240 total grades had improved, despite hundreds of millions of pounds invested.

Top grades no longer have the cachet that derives from rarity. Top grades no longer automatically mean top students. It is obvious: if something is commonplace it is no longer special. However, there is one critical assumption here – the notion that we can accurately measure standards. I have something to say about accuracy in chapters 9 and 10.

Consider the A-level results for 2011. More than half of all the students who sat exams that summer (876,317 total entries) gained at least a B grade, and over a quarter of students gained an A* or A grade! With so many people gaining the top grades, the idea that you've achieved something special is weakened.

But it is worth putting this into perspective by remembering that only a small proportion of the total number of students in formal education go on to gain a grade A at A-level. Half of all students fail to get even five good GCSEs, including Maths and English, never mind good A-levels. Let me paraphrase the depressing statistic delivered by the Secretary of State for Education, Michael Gove: "Look at the numbers of students who gain three A-levels at grade A. Select those who qualify for free school meals and add up the national total. That number is less than the number produced by Eton school alone."

This chapter has dealt with many of the issues that have contributed to the annual rise in exam grades and their impact on confidence in standards. I was personally accountable for ensuring that standards were maintained across different subjects, year-on-year. I was required to comply with a Code of Practice issued by the regulator, Ofqual. (You can find a link to it at *www.examlinks.co.uk*)

The Code of Practice suffers from a number of important weaknesses but it governs the way that teams of examiners must apply their judgements when setting grades. Importantly, the rules were written to deal with single, not modular, exams. It is an important principle that grades awarded to students must reflect their ability and I spent a great deal of my time ensuring that, despite the weaknesses in the process, students got the grades that they deserved. Unfortunately, when the results of separate exam modules are added together there is a tendency for the total grade to be slightly higher than it would have been in a single exam – something known as 'grade inflation'. When modular GCSEs were being introduced in 2009 I raised my deep concerns about this further pressure on standards.

I was issued with guidance to deal with the problems of adding the results of different modules together. This meant that I had to award the grades that every student deserved for each module - but then had to apply adjustments to avoid inflation in the overall grade awarded.

I could not accept this further manipulation of an already complex assessment process. I would no longer be able to claim publicly that the grades awarded reflected the ability of the students that I was responsible for assessing. With considerable regret, I sought a meeting with the Chair and Chief Executive of Ofqual and resigned my authority as Accountable Officer. Not long after I resigned as Managing Director of Edexcel. It is ironic that modular GCSEs are now to be scrapped, albeit for a different reason.

Chapter 9

ON YOUR MARKS...

How exams are marked and graded

Ten years ago, the Chief Executive of the then exams regulator, Dr Ken Boston, set the cat amongst the pigeons when he described the English exam system as a 'cottage industry'. He drew attention to the risky, error-prone process used to assess national exams. Fast forward a decade and new technology has changed the system radically for the better. Key to this change has been the introduction of technology that enabled marking to take place on computer screen. However, the technology that has given so much benefit for GCSE and A-levels is not available for other testing programmes or exams such as SATs.

So how are the main academic exams – GCSEs and A-levels – marked and graded? Let me dispel a few popular myths, starting with this little story, told twice.

MYTH AND REALITY

THE MYTH

Dr James Smith shifted slightly in his old chair. Dust, briefly stirred, danced a slow pattern in the shaft of weak sunlight straining through the study window. For the third time that day he picked up the dog-eared manuscript that carried the essay of Peter Collins. Dr Smith frowned. How could young Collins, surely the most prodigious talent of his year, have submitted such an essay? Why did Collins venture into an academic cul-de-sac in this, the most important of his subjects?

He looked out of the window, unconsciously weighing the manuscript in his hands in a futile gesture of judgement. Twenty years of assessing students. Years that took their toll on his time and demanded his unwavering dedication. Dr Smith did not like loose ends. He always reached for the whole meaning in everything he did.

The manuscript, now placed on the big desk, seemed to look back and mock him, and he frowned again. He drew deeply on his vast experience, turning over each element of the essay, bringing the riot of ideas that it offered together in different ways.

It happened slowly at first, and then built steadily. Reason gradually dawned. Of course! Collins' use of analogy and representation was not misplaced; it was inspirational. The relationships were breathtaking in their concept. Collins was demonstrating a degree of insight that was nothing short of brilliant. Dr Smith's face broke into a wide grin as he glanced quickly through the study window out on to the campus as the chatter of passing students broke the silence. Then he penned his decisive scrawl over Collins' paper and placed it triumphantly on to the pile of marked papers. He looked down at the perfect copperplate manuscript on the next essay and allowed himself a fleeting moment of reflection.

The gold standard was safe in his hands...

THE REALITY

Kevin took the narrow stairs three at a time and spun on his heel at the top landing. The cat, comfortably dozing until then, crouched instinctively and hesitated before springing left to avoid Kevin's feet. One minute later Kevin was in his bedroom starting up his laptop, the glowing screen reflecting dancing highlights on his glasses. He had two good hours before he had to collect his dad from the library and he would put the time to good use. Seconds later the welcome screen invited him to log-on securely and he was ready to begin marking exam questions.

Kevin grimaced as he recalled the previous day. He read again the email from supervisor Stephen chiding him for his error. One miserable error! In marking 870 student responses to question nine, he had made one mistake. The control system, constantly monitoring his performance, had picked this up and reported it to Kevin's supervisor, Stephen.

This was a matter of pride. Kevin knew the importance of accurate marking and worked very hard to understand each mark scheme completely. He had performed well during training and standardisation, and had recorded a perfect performance during his marking of question 15 over the last two weeks – and he had been perfect on question nine too, until yesterday. He knew that Stephen would have personally re-checked much of his marking of question nine using the so called back-reading system. Stephen always followed up every apparent problem.

Question nine flicked up on the screen. Focus! There would be no more errors for the control system to find, and nothing for Stephen to do but congratulate him. Plus the money he was earning would come in very handy for his holiday in Spain later this year.

Kevin smiled as his mobile phone rang and the caller ID was displayed. Supervisor Stephen was calling, no doubt ready with his vast teaching and marking experience to encourage, chide and support. He grinned and thumbed his mobile.

"Stephen, hi."

Maybe you think a typical examiner is someone like old Dr Smith, but Kevin is much nearer the truth. Armed with a laptop and an internet connection, the chances are that Kevin is more accurate and consistent than Dr Smith ever was. Significantly, Kevin is liable to be a recent graduate in the examined subject and may not even be a teacher.

Who Marks Exams?

Would you prefer a Dr Smith or a Kevin to mark your exams? Would you be happy for a recent graduate, rather than an experienced teacher, to assess your work? The fact is non-teachers have been marking exams – or at least parts of exams – for years. And do you know what? They generally do a fantastic job. So who are the examiners, markers and moderators that pass judgement on your best efforts and have a major say in deciding your future? A key principle of the UK's exam system is that you shouldn't know them – and they shouldn't know you. One of the rules is that examiners must not have any connection with the school, college or students whose work they mark.

Since the introduction of the national curriculum, the business of marking and grading exams has become much more formal and structured. Examiners are hired through press advertisements and apply directly to the exam boards. The main exams take place three times a year: summer (the largest), winter (in January, covering mainly A-levels), and autumn (in November, often with a proportion of re-sits). Exam boards recruit separately for each of these exam series and train every examiner and moderator for each exam; so examiners are contracted and trained three times a year! The terms *examiner* and *marker* are generally interchangeable when describing the people who assess GCSEs and A-levels. Controlled assessments and work produced for vocational qualifications like BTEC are assessed directly by teachers and lecturers in schools and colleges. But samples of this work are then checked for consistency and accuracy by moderators, who are hired by the exam boards.

Most exam questions these days are carefully constructed and accompanied by strict guidelines, known as mark schemes, which specify how marks are to be allocated. Some questions, like long essays, demand considerable subject knowledge and judgement and tend to be marked by more senior or experienced markers. Shorter questions, which count for far fewer marks, don't need the same level of subject expertise. Until 2003 all examiners and moderators were people who had taught in schools or colleges, most of whom were still teaching the current syllabus. Retired teachers and supply teachers made up the rest, with the chance of earning £600 to £1,000 for a typical summer marking session. From 2003 onwards, when the regulator opened the door to change, the exam board Edexcel implemented new technology enabling hand-written exam papers to be scanned by industrial-sized scanners, turning each paper into a digital file. These could then be electronically cut into smaller files to separate individual questions and answers.

This meant that answers to individual questions could be made available online, so instead of marking 300 whole exam papers, examiners were able to mark answers to a single question. All this was done via secure internet systems like those used by banks to protect your personal finances online. Special software enabled examiners to, quite literally, 'mark' the answers on screen. Questions were classified according to how difficult they were to assess. For example, if the only correct answer to a question is the number '10' and the student is to be awarded one mark for '10' and no mark for any other response, then you don't need a teacher or anyone with in-depth subject knowledge to mark that; you can train others to do the work.

As a result, a small army of so-called 'clerical markers' is appointed every year to mark simple exam questions. Millions of questions are marked in Australia to enable continuous 24 hour operations! Many of these markers have had a university education. Skilled personnel are essential to the success of any exam programme and the exam boards compete for good people, offering cash and other benefits. During the early 2000s some subjects, such as Religious Studies, experienced many critical shortages, driving up bonus awards and other enticements. But the work is very hard and must meet strict deadlines.

Despite the changes, experienced teachers remain the backbone of the system and they mark questions that require a good degree of subject knowledge or a great deal of professional judgement. Teachers are willing to do so for two main reasons: they get paid for it and they gain a better appreciation of how their students are tested. It's also the case that some exams are still assessed in the traditional way with a red pen and a pile of student manuscripts. These all require teachers to take charge. Many professional qualifications are marked by experts in this way, although professional bodies are also moving towards forms of so-called e-assessment.

HOW MARKING WORKS – THE NUTS AND BOLTS

PAPER CHASE

The traditional, non-computer based method of marking exams saw millions of manuscripts criss-crossing the country in postal vans every summer. The exam papers were collected from schools and colleges and delivered to the homes of about 40,000 examiners. Coursework brought its own problems – I've seen special arrangements being made for a model of Sydney Harbour Bridge to be sent to a moderator to be assessed.

In the traditional way, examiners:

- ✓ Are recruited based on their qualifications and experience

- ✓ Attend training days in person to learn the mark scheme for the paper

- ✓ Are tested on their ability to mark actual papers and rejected if they fail to meet minimum standards

- ✓ Are sent about 300 exam papers from schools, colleges and other exam centres

- ✓ Check that attendance registers from schools and colleges match the exam papers they have actually received

- ✓ Send off hand written forms to report problems

- ✓ Mark the exam papers in the pile

- ✓ Add up the total mark for each paper and copy it on to a summary form, which is later posted to the exam board

- ✓ After they've marked a certain number of papers, post a sample of their marked exam papers to the exam board to check for accuracy and consistency

- ✓ Receive confirmation from the exam board to continue– or to stop marking if the quality wasn't good enough

- ✓ Post off two more samples to be checked during the marking period

- ✓ Post exam papers on completion of marking to the exam board

- ✓ Fill in and post forms for payment and expenses

AN 'E' WITH EVERYTHING – MARKING USING COMPUTERS

A lot of nonsense has been written about the use of computers in marking. Computers enable trained, skilled human beings to mark student responses to questions faster. They also enable a level of accuracy and consistency that is significantly better than traditional methods. Let me describe just a few of the improvements in accuracy:

- ✓ Extensive trials conducted by Edexcel in 2003 and validated by the regulator showed that examiner judgement was at least as good when marking on screen

- ✓ There are no human errors caused by adding up question scores and copying totals on to summary sheets – a common reason for wrong results in the past

- ✓ Electronic quality control systems monitor real marking and are vastly superior to the old sample method where the examiner could 'select' some of his or her own marked papers for scrutiny

- ✓ The ability to manage workloads on examiners avoids the habitual crises in the traditional system that caused errors through marking under time pressure

- ✓ There are no administrative distractions such as checking attendance registers or missing papers

- ✓ Marking individual questions instead of whole exam papers enables the most experienced and skilled examiners to focus exclusively on the toughest questions

- ✓ All of the support materials are available instantly on screen

✓ Any issue can be flashed instantly to the whole marking team on screen and instructions can be modified quickly.

On this last point, one exam paper in 2000 had a question asking students to list practical uses for a hypodermic syringe. Unfortunately, students affected by the massive press coverage of the Dr Harold Shipman murder case suggested 'murder' as a use. Of course the mark scheme did not list that as a practical use! If on-screen marking had been available, the problem could have been raised quickly and new instructions flashed to every examiner on how to deal with the unexpected response.

Only a tiny fraction of student responses is measured directly by computer and these are multiple choice questions. Students complete specially designed exam papers that are read digitally without the need for any human being to look at them. Multiple-choice is used only where it is considered to be the best assessment method available.

Today many GCSEs and A-levels are assessed using on-screen marking. Technology has transformed the process. Here's a typical summary of how it works. Examiners:

✓ Are recruited and issued with contracts online

✓ Are trained and tested online

✓ Must attain minimum standards for each separate question

✓ Gain accreditation to mark nominated questions

✓ Mark anonymous student responses to questions on a secure internet link

✓ Are prevented from copying or retaining any data

✓ Begin marking, with the marks awarded transmitted automatically to the exam board

✓ Are checked for quality and accuracy online in real time as special tests are secreted in the programme

✓ Use online support and instruction systems, with no paper in sight

This method is possible because completed exam papers are all sent directly from schools to a single processing centre to be scanned. Student answers are captured digitally, identified and stored ready for electronic distribution to approved markers. The process is very fast, but the real benefits come with much greater marking accuracy and no risk of papers being lost in the post. It also means that the whole exam paper of each student is marked by several different examiners, who specialise in marking a limited number of questions. This helps to eliminate bias.

THE TOP TEAM

Every exam subject at every level has a hierarchy of markers and examiners. It usually looks something like this.

The *Chair of Examiners* is the top man or woman responsible for the professional running of the whole process. This includes setting the exam questions, training examiners and deciding what marks are worth what grades. Most Chairs are not employed directly by exam boards, but are senior figures in their fields, such as very experienced heads of department.

They have to be good leaders and managers and have the highest integrity. Chair appointments carry a lot of prestige and holders can earn fees from external activities in addition to negotiated contracts with exam boards.

The *Chief Examiner* comes next and is responsible for the conduct of the exam itself, directing training and supervising marking standards. Chief Examiners must mark some exam papers themselves. Where advanced technology is used, Chief Examiners contribute to the massive quality control programmes.

The *Principal Examiner* is next and heads up the creation of the exam paper, taking it from first principles through drafting to final publication. This work is done in secret and can take a long time. Principal Examiners must also ensure that substitute exam papers are prepared in case of a security breach.

The *Reviser* reviews exam papers, looking for ambiguity or inconsistency. Language is very important in setting exam questions. Over the years there have been several instances when students could have tackled a question well but were prevented by a word that they did not understand that had little to do with the subject.

The *Scrutineer* works through the exam paper in advance, checking for problems or possible misunderstandings and ensures that the time allowed is appropriate.

After these important positions comes a vast array of others with titles such as Examiners, General Markers, Principal Moderators, Assistants, and so on. You get the picture;

every exam is overseen by a massive bureaucracy working to a strict set of rules overseen by a regulator.

This process works very well, but is not completely foolproof, as publicity around errors in some exam papers during 2011 showed. In addition to the work of the top team, exam boards have stringent quality checks, which really should prevent errors from taking place.

A 'B' OR NOT A 'B' - THAT IS THE QUESTION (HOW EXAMINERS SET GRADES)

How do examiners decide what grade your work will receive? This is a complex process, but let's begin with a really important assumption. The setting of 'grade boundaries', as this job is known, is based on the notion that experienced examiners 'know' what your effort is worth. These experts can pick up an exam paper in their subject and say, "that's worth a grade C", or whatever. As an engineer entering the world of exams a decade ago, I found the absence of some form of fixed reference quite difficult to accept. So the first point to note is that the different grades are set by experts who 'know' about levels of performance. It is these knowing, professional judgements that determine whether the standard is being held year-on-year. Experts can also refer to published grade descriptions that set out what a student should demonstrate in order to be worthy of the award of the grade.

After the exams have been marked, the top team of examiners meets in committee to set the different grade boundaries. They are helped by looking at exam papers from previous years, reviewing statistics of grades awarded in the past, and an analysis of current results data.

For GCSE they then start with the critical C grade; let's say it's expected to be at about 40 marks for a particular exam. They then inspect samples of exam papers with marks above and below 40 – say from 46 to 35. This way they reach agreement that no student with less than 36 marks is worth a C and all papers above 46 marks are worthy of a grade B. But, between these two marks – in this case 36 and 46 – some may disagree about what grade an exam paper should be given. Their job is to thrash out an agreement on where the best 'threshold' should be for a grade C for that particular exam. After doing so, they repeat the process at key grades until they have established boundaries for every grade.

Once each committee has finished, the exam board runs a computer simulation to see whether this has led to changes to the annual performance tables. Remember that exam boards aren't just responsible for giving every single student an accurate grade in every subject, but must also ensure that standards are maintained over time. If the outcome is that more students achieved higher grades, there must be evidence to justify the decision. Exam committees must be able to judge whether the current exam paper is harder or easier than last year and reflect that in the grade boundaries they set. Every single exam paper – and piece of controlled assessment – goes through this process or one very similar, although technology means that these committees don't always meet face to face. So does the system ensure that standards are held year-on-year, and that the grade boundary decisions are accurate?

Probably...

Helped by mark schemes, exam boards strive for consistency so that if the same question was marked by ten different examiners the overall mark awarded would be similar. Note that I said 'similar', not 'the same'. There is an unwritten acceptance that, at best, markers can only achieve plus or minus half a grade in consistency when marking a whole paper.

However, a great deal of effort goes into designing question papers and marking exams. Grades are ultimately set using the judgement of 'people who know about standards'. Of course judgements are potentially easier to make with low level Maths papers where marks awarded tend to be more precise. Long essays, where marks are awarded for style or other imprecise factors, are much more difficult. However, the fact remains that every exam paper demands judgement and the accusations about dumbing down apply as much to Maths as they do to English.

Many other countries take a different approach, setting and secretly testing each exam question in advance. This means that grades are set on the basis of simple student scores, without the need for post-exam analysis. We cannot do this because we run exams on an industrial scale, with about 40,000 different questions being set across our vast range of GCSE and GCE exam papers.

Chapter 10

RESULTS DAY AND BEYOND

Every year examiners are put under enormous pressure to mark millions of exam papers in a very short space of time. Hundreds of thousands of candidates have been told the day on which they will receive their results – and the wrath of a vengeful media will fall on the head of any exam board that misses the deadline for even a handful of students. But while exam boards overwhelmingly meet the results day deadline, things can – and do – go wrong. Think about it...

✓ About 40,000 markers have to be recruited, trained, assessed and allocated papers or questions to mark

✓ The examiners are themselves graded according to their competence, with more experienced supervising markers managing a team and carrying out quality assurance checks. This means some examiners are stopped from marking and questions have to be re-marked by others

✓ Modular exams mean that examiners are often marking only a part of part the whole, which has to be totalled from all of the separate elements

✓ Taking all of the questions to be marked from all of the different subjects in all of the different exams, each summer examiners mark an estimated 250 million questions!

The scale of the task is colossal, so it isn't surprising that things sometimes go wrong. As a candidate you sit your exam and your paper is collected. You then have to wait two to three months for the results as the examiners go through the painstaking process described in chapter 9. So after a long and sometimes anxious wait, the big day comes and you receive your results. You open up the slip of paper with baited breath to find...what? If you receive the grade you were expecting or hoping for – or have done even better than that – you feel fantastic. You can probably remember the TV bulletins and newspaper photos of embracing, happy students every results day.

But what if you've done worse than you were expecting – or even much worse? What if you think you've been awarded the wrong grade, which means you won't be able to do the A-level you'd wanted, or impress a prospective employer or get into your first choice university? What can you do about it? Every year, thousands of students face the disappointment of poor grades, although they're usually a long way away from the nearest TV camera or telephoto lens.

A formal process exists to address problems like this, known as *Enquiry about Results*. But before we look at how this works, let's try to understand why mistakes happen in the first place.

WHY YOU MIGHT RECEIVE THE WRONG GRADE

THE MARKING WAS INACCURATE

Despite the best efforts of exam boards to control the quality and performance of thousands of markers, they don't always get it right. Your exam paper might have been marked by an examiner who made errors.

ADMINISTRATIVE COCK UP

Despite the advances with new technology in some areas, many examiners still have to add up individual question marks manually and then enter them onto a summary sheet, which is used as the basis for your grade. Simple adding errors occur, so if your mark total is wrong, the chances are that the grade you are awarded will be wrong, too.

MODULES HAVE NOT BEEN 'CASHED IN'

Remember that modular exams require schools, colleges and other learning providers to 'cash in' the results of each of the modules you've taken. Unfortunately this is a common error. I know of cases where an exam board has results for all of the modules for a pupil or group of pupils, but they haven't been cashed in and the exam board can't act because all of the school's staff have gone on holiday.

YOUR EXAM PAPER HAS BEEN LOST OR DESTROYED

With more and more exams marked online, this possibility is rarer than it used to be, but it can and does happen. Each year post office vans are stolen, robbed or involved in accidents. Parcels go to the wrong address. Some examiners will move house at a critical moment, become involved in a domestic crisis, die, go insane or leave the exam papers on a train. These real examples are all very rare, but they can and do happen. When they do, exam boards estimate the result they think you would have received based on evidence from other exams you have taken and estimates from your school, college or provider. In most cases this happens before you are given your grade, but you must be told that your grade is an estimate. Again, you might appeal, but remember that your teacher or tutor will take no action if he or she agrees with the estimate.

Your Candidate Number Has Been Duplicated

Every candidate is given a unique identity number by the exam board setting the particular exam. This number is critical if you have module results that need to be added up to give a final score. Sometimes students end up with more than one reference number (for example if they move to a new school or college). Teachers (or more likely, the exams officers in schools and colleges) allocate these numbers. As a result, your total score may be incorrect if it only reflects your results for one reference number but not the other. Sorting out this problem requires skilled detective work by the exam board.

What You Can Do If Things Go Wrong

If you believe you've been the victim of poor marking or an administrative mistake, the problem has to be sorted out formally through your learning provider, school or college, who will have to contact the relevant exam board. What this means is that you must have their support if you are to have any chance of a successful appeal through the process known as Enquiry about Results.

HOW TO COMPLAIN ABOUT YOUR RESULTS

Exam boards offer three services to anyone unhappy with their grades. In each case, you need the support of your school, college or learning provider.

- ✓ **Service 1** – a clerical check of your paper to ensure that all of the questions have been marked and that the total has been added up correctly.

- ✓ **Service 2** – a full re-mark of the paper by a senior examiner and a clerical check of the total. A-level papers can be given a priority service.

- ✓ **Service 3** – a review of the moderation of work that has been assessed by your school, college or learning provider, usually for coursework or controlled assessment.

Figure 11

If you have a problem your first action should be to contact your teacher or the specialist administrator called the exams officer. Do this immediately because teaching staff usually disappear very quickly after results are issued. Think about the possible cause of the problem and ask for an Enquiry about Results. Three different types of enquiry service exist and these are shown in Figure 11.

Each of these enquires attracts a fee and you must request it by a deadline. Fees vary across different exam boards and for different services, and your school should be able to advise you before proceeding. If the enquiry is just for you, then you may have to pay, but if the enquiry is on behalf of a whole class, then the school or college will pay the fee. If the enquiry is upheld the fee is waived. Remember that your teacher, lecturer or tutor makes the final decision to submit an enquiry, so you need him or her to support you. If he or she thinks that your grade was fair then they may not take any action, so be persistent.

One problem students often face is that many exam results are issued in the summer when your school or college may have shut up shop after dispensing the results. To be fair, many schools and colleges make a big effort to make someone available during this stressful period, but don't assume that's the case. You should find out in advance who will be on hand for the period after results are released and make sure you have their contact details. Many teachers and lecturers don't like being part of this support process and are often reluctant to begin the necessary administration. Remember, they must make a judgement about your appeal and can simply refuse to submit one.

Enquiries about results can be made on behalf of individuals or a whole class. The key is to be persistent. If all else fails you can try to reach the exam board directly, but its staff will resist taking action without a teacher's formal submission and their telephone numbers usually connect you to call centres that are under orders to avoid putting you through directly.

One route you might try is to reach to the Accountable Officer in the exam board – he or she is responsible for the conduct of the whole exam process and will take action if your school or college has gone into hiding. How do you reach the Accountable Officer? Exam boards are like many other large organisations, such as energy suppliers and water boards, employing call centres to avoid phone calls going directly into the organisation. However, they nearly always put a contact name and number for the senior person who looks after their media profile and news on their web site. Call them and ask for the name of the Accountable Officer on some pretext and you will have a name to call directly. Although exam board staff can be difficult to reach there is a very strong culture of student support. If you can get through the defences you will probably get help, but you have to be realistic about your chances of getting through.

Failing that, the next source of help is the regulator. Again, their staff will attempt to funnel you through the established process and point you to the school or college, but be persistent. The regulator will not overturn an individual judgement; their intervention is limited to observing that proper procedures have been followed. Thus your strongest argument is to complain that due process has not been followed. For example, you believe that an error is being overlooked or that your requests are being denied. Unfortunately, working through a combination of regulator, learning provider and exam board can be tortuous and slow. Keep reminding the regulator that their prime purpose is to look after the interests of students and that lethargy and slow procedures are no excuse for inaction on your behalf.

If all else fails you can refer your enquiry to the independent Examinations Appeals Board. Go to their website to read about the appeals made, but the number of appeals heard annually is very low, with just 24 for the whole of 2010. Judgements are usually made long after critical career, further or higher education decisions have to be made.

ARE YOU SPECIAL?

When you took your exam, did a fire alarm destroy your concentration? Or did you forget to take your hay fever tablets and couldn't stop sneezing throughout the whole two hours? Or did your pet dog die the day before? These and many, many other factors that might affect your performance in an exam can be taken into account by exam boards through something called 'Special Considerations'.

This gives exam boards some leeway to make adjustments to your final result and is intended to compensate for unforeseen events and circumstances. A long list of rules and regulations governs the judgements and allowances that they make. For example, terminal illness of a member of the immediate family or a serious domestic crisis might gain an additional 5% of marks. A recently broken limb or witness of a distressing event might gain 3% more marks.

I recall one memorable request in a long letter from the invigilator in a South Yorkshire school setting out in some detail the circumstances of an event during a Physics exam. The letter was accompanied by a diagram showing the layout of the room with table numbers and candidate identities. A dotted line meandered around a group of tables near the back of the room. This dotted line traced the journey of a pet frog, which had escaped from the pocket of a luckless student resulting in hoots of laughter punctuated by screams and abandoned papers. The frog survived, the owner was chastened and my team set about assessing the special considerations. As with all of these incidents the team had to judge the impact on each student, taking the length of distraction and the unsettling affect on concentration, resulting in an increased mark.

The JCQ (Joint Council for Qualifications) acts as a kind of trade body for the main exam boards and publishes the rules governing special considerations (and access arrangements, highlighted in chapter 6). Check *www. examlinks.co.uk* for a link. While this is well worth a read, the current guide is 74 pages long and is not for the faint hearted.

One crucial fact to bear in mind about special considerations is that you can't take action on your own. You must be supported by your school, college or learning provider, and their staff must apply on your behalf. Make sure you get your facts straight before approaching the school, particularly if your claim has to be backed by a report from a doctor or other professional.

PUTTING YOUR RESULTS IN PERSPECTIVE

To put the issue of wrong grades into perspective, here's an extract from a recent regulator's report:

"Following the release of results for the summer 2010 examinations series, there were 171,700 enquiries about results. For GCSE, there were a total of 24,200 subject grade changes following enquiry, representing 0.40 per cent of all GCSE subject entries. For GCE, there were a total of 10,500 subject grade changes following enquiry, representing 0.47 per cent of all GCE subject entries."

Whilst these statistics cover GCSE and A-Level, similar procedures apply to all other qualifications, including vocational and other awards.

Of course, if you're one of the 0.4% of students whose results were changed because of a marker error or administrative cock up, getting a sense of perspective will be difficult. This is especially true if your first choice university's conditional offer was removed because you were given the wrong grade, or your hoped-for career path dissolved before your eyes. One factor that might help is that you can be sure in the knowledge that exam boards act swiftly to remove poor examiners on evidence of poor performance, with several dismissals every year. In turn the regulator monitors exam board performance and requires them to take action to put right any problems.

One final point. Although it is a rare occurrence, exam boards sometimes produce exam papers with errors. These errors can be, for example, numbers with incorrect values resulting in 'impossible' questions, or words that serve to confuse. Page numbers and references can be mixed up. Tables and diagrams, often produced at a late stage in the creation of an exam paper, account for a measurable source of errors. As a candidate taking the exam, perhaps confident of the subject being tested, it can be very unsettling to come up against a question that you should be able to tackle well, but that does not make sense. Exam boards don't write trick questions and try very hard to avoid ambiguity that could cause confusion. Exam papers should provide an opportunity for you to demonstrate what you know and what skills you have developed; they should not embody intellectual tricks (unless the exam is seeking to measure your analytical skills in some way by setting puzzles – and you should be expecting puzzles).

An error in an exam paper is a very serious incident in the running of an exam, and will attract the attention of the regulator – there is a current initiative aimed at fining boards that make errors. Exam boards have a series of procedures that they must follow in order to compensate for the impact of an error. For example, a question might be removed from the paper and the overall total marks for the exam reduced accordingly. Examiners will estimate the time wasted by candidates and take into account the anxiety created by the error, and may add marks to each candidate score. This procedure might appear to be imprecise, but examination teams draw on experience and circumstantial evidence to reach an agreed plan of corrective action, and record that action in a formal report. The examination team will also carefully monitor each Enquiry about Results to check that their corrective action has covered all of the issues. After all that, the overall candidate performance in that paper in terms of grades awarded will be closely scrutinised and compared with that of other exam boards offering the same subject, and of other examinations – all under the eye of the regulator.

Overall, though, given the tens of millions of transactions that characterise examinations each year, perhaps the relatively low proportion of amended grades indicates that the system, though imperfect, is working pretty well.

Chapter 11

IN CONCLUSION

Where do we go from here?

D uring the last weeks of 2011 a series of articles in The Telegraph accused exam boards of giving insider secrets to teachers. These articles added to a negative historical perspective and heaped more scorn on the exam boards, contributing to the continuing unease that many feel about the integrity of the exam system. In this book I have tried to explain what really goes on so that future changes might be better informed. If radical changes are to be made to our exam system they should be made in the light of reality.

Perhaps the single greatest failure of the exam system is that it has presided over a loss of public confidence. Restoration of confidence in universities, employers, students and parents is paramount. Confidence will only be restored if exam outcomes are intuitively sensible and transparent. Changes will have to embrace teaching and learning as well as the way that exams are set and run. The impact of league tables on classroom behaviour should not be ignored.

The exam system in England, Wales and Northern Ireland is, despite its faults, one that we should be proud of. It has a high degree of integrity, underpinned by the honesty and professionalism of the overwhelming majority of people who participate. Our qualifications have international stature. However, the exam programme is designed for people who work in education; for those who teach and assess. It has an internal focus. League tables significantly influence how teachers teach and demonstrate the classic consequence of the measurement affecting the outcome. There is no real voice for the customers: students, parents, guardians, universities and employers. The regulator has in the past fallen short of setting customer service standards that have transparent meaning for everyone who has a stake in the system.

The exam system is far too complex, with confusing rules about levels and outcomes. The way that GCSEs and A-levels are graded has undermined confidence in qualifications, especially at the top. Student performance statistics published each year instinctively give the impression of dumbing down, and mask the fact that the improvements in grades should have been even better year-on-year. Yet overall student attainment is poor, with the award of five good GCSEs stubbornly low in state schools, and only a tiny fraction attaining three A-levels at grade A.

Added to this is the massive burden of exams taken each year. In a single summer, exam boards have to deal with around one quarter of a billion student responses to questions and tasks. (That's from 15.7 million exam papers marked and 8.2 million awards made in summer 2011). We run exams on an industrial scale but organise it with a staff room perspective. It is a tribute to the teams of exam officers in schools and colleges, the exam boards' organisations, and the army of examiners and markers that so few errors occur.

I believe that we need to put real pressure on our teaching and learning practice if we are to improve public confidence and student achievement. You should note that I did not say that we should put pressure on schools and colleges; they are already under severe pressure to achieve league table points and to meet Ofsted demands. More of the same will yield only diminishing returns. And isn't it curious that we have separate bodies for assessing teaching and learning in schools and for assessing students.? Ofsted and Ofqual don't seem to have many formal links, yet they could learn much from each other.

Here then are some strategies that might help to bring about some of the changes that are needed.

Consumer Pressure

This book is deliberately intended to help concerned parents and students (and concerned teachers) to challenge the exam system. Parents and students should not accept the status-quo. Customer pressure is a powerful agent of change and is evident in almost every area of industry and commerce. In Edexcel I offered a free service to students and parents on results days, showing how close each award was to an adjacent grade, and encouraged students to challenge my assessment. I produced a free, detailed analysis of how well every question in each exam performed, encouraging teachers to complain about questions that performed poorly. I created analyses of how well every student understood the subject under study; how well every cohort and class understood the subject; how well every teacher taught; and how well each school or college performed year-on-year. The analyses were produced in great detail showing precisely what was learnt and what was not.

Sadly, very few teachers and school management teams used the data. I showed the analyses to school governors and to the regulator, but they declined to make use of them. Poor teachers and poor schools carry on as before with the same shortcomings evident year after year. These analyses were never made available to the general public because I did not want to undermine the exam system, or to give opportunistic journalists the ammunition to draw spurious conclusions. Exposing Edexcel to external criticism was one of the strategies used in driving up quality and accuracy. We put ourselves on the line and had to live up to the pressure. Educationalists seem to me to be a long way from openly inviting constructive criticism. Very few teachers are dismissed for incompetence, and I was able to see the same depressing class outcomes again and again in the analyses.

Consumerism is a powerful agent of change; it should be introduced into the exam system, in a framework set out by the regulator, Ofqual.

A Single Exam Board?

I should start by declaring bias given my past experience in Edexcel.

There is a popular belief that competition amongst exam boards leads to the writing of easy exam questions in order to win business from one another, and as a consequence, pass rates rise each year. If that is true, then the regulator has consistently failed to spot it, since each examination outcome is scrutinised and reviewed every time exams are taken. In chapter 8 I outlined the reasons behind the steady rise in national exam grades; they are almost entirely due to government education policy and a determination to improve exam results. Modular exams, greater choice, coursework, re-sits, tier changes and exam practice in schools have made better exam results possible.

If exam boards are using easy questions to win business from one another their efforts seem to be in vain. The market share of qualifications won by exam boards has remained stubbornly constant, varying by only a few percentage points each year. Schools and colleges stay resolutely loyal to their existing exam board, but I should of course remind you that schools and colleges don't make single organisational decisions; each subject head chooses independently. In 2008 and 2009 Edexcel investigated a phenomenon called 'churn' where it was noticed that there were a number of significant 'losses and gains' in some subjects. We saw that much of this churn was due to subject heads moving to a new school and taking their preferred exam board with them.

A single exam board run by a quango is unlikely to innovate and adopt modern management and technology; an example of this is the current arrangement for SATs: a bureaucratic, risk-laden paper empire. A single exam board will not change teaching behaviour and the pressure to teach to the test; it might make such behaviour even more determined. A single exam board will not experience the commercial pressure on cost management. Although there are four exam boards competing in England and Wales, schools only purchase once.

If a single board is to be introduced we must take the opportunity to change the way that exams are organised to recognise the massive scale of assessment in this country – it cannot be left to people whose operational experience is limited to the classroom.

STANDARDS

The current system of setting standards suffers from fundamental problems: measurement depends on experts who 'know' what grades actual student responses are worth by reading completed exam papers; there are no external references except the history of what has gone before

Grade boundaries were fixed some years ago and cannot effectively provide a reference for standards over time because teaching and learning have improved (and arguably so has teaching to the test); changes to exam structures such as the introduction of modules and 'C-friendly' questions have been introduced; and there are pressures on the whole system to demonstrate success.

The current system does not effectively discriminate; it does not rank-order the attainment of students. Too many candidates attain top grades, undermining the achievement of the very best. The A* grade is a temporary fix. Does the A** grade appear at some time in the future?

AN ALTERNATIVE STRATEGY

We could address the issue of standards over time and the disquiet about dumbing down by setting up an independent panel that would decompose each exam question structure and type, and conduct a substantial national survey based on student responses to separate questions rather than whole papers. Accurate, repeatable marking depends on the availability of an unambiguous mark scheme; one that effectively caters for any examiner discretion. This panel would draw a statistically significant sample of student responses from the latest set of exams and publish independent findings. It is essential, however, that the panel is not dominated by educationalists, and that its members include a range of individuals from science, industry and commerce. Education should not measure itself.

Exam boards could simply rank-order students in addition to awarding grades. The fact that there would have to be a separate list for each board does not matter. Students could be placed in their percentile position in each case. If this was implemented, exam awards might read, for example: Grade A; 83 percentile AQA, or Grade A; 70 percentile Edexcel. The first student gained an A grade and was ranked at the 83% percentile point, and the second at the 73% percentile point. The first student did better. The percentile point indicates the relative performance of each student compared with his or her peers.

This approach maintains the current system in essence but adds the task of the independent panel. Of course we could simply go back the old system and just rank order students saving £millions in the difficult and expensive task of setting grades.

Understanding Standards

In Chapter 8 I described the problem of language in the communication of standards. Educationalists define a 'standard' as the set hurdles for grade A, B and so on. But when we see an exam set with grades A to G, we intuitively expect that a few students will achieve grade A; it simply does not feel right when large numbers attain the top grade. The public, and that includes employers and universities, needs to be able to discriminate the very best from the average and the poor. In the real world we want to regard grade A as 'excellent' and if almost a third of candidates are awarded an 'A' in an exam, then we cannot accept that they are all excellent. Excellence means rare, few and exceptional.

Someone has to take the lead in communicating the performance of students in a meaningful way. My suggestion is that the regulator, Ofqual – and its counterparts in Wales and Northern Ireland - should take up this challenge using language that everyone with an interest can relate to, not just educational specialists. Student achievement in state schools remains relatively poor, with significant numbers failing to reach the expected standard. The attainment of disadvantaged students, usually categorised as receiving free school meals, is disastrous. News reporting would have us believe that good exam grades are easy to achieve with pass rates ever climbing and approaching 100%, yet the reality is very different. Without some concerted action, confidence in exams will continue to decline.

I am sure that this book won't be popular amongst many educationalists. I expect to be criticised. I expect that inaccuracies will be observed. I wrote it to reach out to ordinary people and to encourage them to challenge the exam system.

I hope that the challenge makes our great exam system better.

Lightning Source UK Ltd.
Milton Keynes UK
UKOW051516050312

188388UK00001B/274/P